Secondary Mathematics and Special Educational Needs

Harry Daniels and Julia Anghileri

CASSELL

Titles in the Special Needs in Ordinary Schools series
Meeting Special Needs in Ordinary Schools: An Overview
   (2nd edition)
Assessing Special Educational Needs
Management for Special Needs
Reappraising Special Needs Education

Forthcoming:

Educating the Able
Mobility for Special Needs
Working with Parents of Children with Special Educational Needs

Cassell   387 Park Avenue South
Wellington House   New York
125 Strand   NY 10016–8810
London WC2R OBB   USA

First published 1995

British Library Cataloguing-in-Publication Data
A catalogue record for this book is available from the British Library

ISBN 0–304–32800–6 (hardback)
    0–304–32798–0 (paperback)

Typeset by Colset Private Limited, Singapore
Printed and bound in Great Britain by
Biddles Ltd, Guildford and King's Lynn

Contents

Editorial foreword

It is now commonplace to assert that special educational needs can be created and complicated by an inappropriate curriculum and teaching methods. But such claims have a long history when it comes to competence in simple arithmetic. Generations of otherwise able people, including many who have distinguished themselves in other fields, do not seem at all embarrassed by their inability to carry out the most rudimentary calculations. It seems quite acceptable in most circles to blame 'bad teaching' for failure to cope with fractions or percentages or having an emotional block where numbers are concerned. Even when teachers are not blamed, 'being no good with numbers' is socially acceptable, compared with difficulties in reading and literacy.

Why is having problems in learning and using basic mathematics acceptable in our society and in the eduction system as a whole? How many schools still accept that poor mathematical performance often co-exists with above average performance in other areas of the curriculum? And how do we compare with our European, North American and Asian 'competitors' in this respect? What proportion of Japanese or Korean children have significant learning difficulties where maths is concerned?

The Cockcroft report (1982) aimed to bring about a radical reform of the maths curriculum and its standing in schools and in society. Although overtaken by the National Curriculum and its never-ending revisions, the questions posed by Cockcroft seem more important than ever. They concern the importance of mathematical understanding and skills both for the intellectual development of pupils and for the requirements of society, as well as the need to convince pupils of the usefulness and the excitement of mathematics as a tool and as a process of enquiry.

From a special needs point of view, the latest proposals for the revisions to the maths curriculum have sought to ensure that the curriculum is accessible to all pupils at level 1 and that the programmes of study at all levels cater for the whole range of pupils in schools. Whether they will succeed in convincing teachers as well as pupils remains to be seen. The key issues are still concerned with access, progression, coherence and continuity. In the meantime, we remain as a nation in a state of profound mathematical underfunctioning. The publication of this book also coincides with the implementation of the *Code of Practice for the Identification and Assessment of Special Educational Needs*, perhaps the most important initiative since the Warnock report some 15 years ago.

But what implications do these developments have for reducing mathematical difficulties and failures, given the priority given by schools and support services to reading and behaviour problems in identifying and meeting special educational needs? Will support services inside and outside schools be mobilized to prevent and intervene to support children with significant learning difficulties in mathematics? It seems that mathematics teachers have in general accepted full responsibility for meeting the needs of pupils with mathematical difficulties and have relied on their own experience and expertise.

The book could therefore hardly be more timely. It does not confine itself to discussing better methods of teaching children with difficulties to acquire and use mathematical skills. It is also concerned with the prevention of such difficulties occurring in the first place, and with improving the quality of mathematics teaching for all pupils. It exemplifies once again that what is good teaching for children with special educational needs is good teaching for all children.

Professor Peter Mittler
School of Education
University of Manchester
August 1994

Prologue

This book is concerned with difficulty in learning mathematics in secondary schools. The intention is to provide a discussion which is of value to special needs teachers who know relatively little about current practice in mathematics education and also to mathematics teachers who are unfamiliar with recent developments in special needs education and anyone who is interested in the provision for pupils with Special Educational Needs (SEN) in mainstream schools. As such it may be read in different ways by readers with differing experiences. There are important points in common to both mathematics and SEN teachers that make us feel that it is worth writing one book together rather than one book each. We intend to address the pedagogical and curriculum content implications of difficulty in learning and have avoided the temptation of writing both disability specific and mathematics curriculum content specific chapters. Our strategy has been to pursue pedagogic themes and to select examples and vignettes which are referenced to specific areas of interest and concern.

Much has been written to the effect that it is inappropriate to think of educational need solely in terms of individual children. Inflexibility in existing provision for mathematics in mainstream schools will affect the special needs requirements of pupils. The Dearing Report (Dearing, 1993) states:

> It is estimated that some 20% of pupils following the National Curriculum will at some time in their school career have Special Educational Needs. For many of these pupils the difficulties will be minor and short-lived. Others will have profound and multiple learning disabilities. Given this range, it is impossible to prescribe a curriculum which will meet the particular needs of every pupil. What the National Curriculum should and must do is to allow teachers and schools to meet the particular needs of pupils with Special Educational Needs in ways which they judge to be relevant. Only when this is the case can we justifiably claim that the National Curriculum is a curriculum for all.

This book will accordingly explore school, classroom and curriculum issues along with those of intervention at the level of the individual. We adopt a position which argues for teaching which is responsive to individual understanding and provides a balance of challenge and satisfaction in mathematics learning at all levels. If teachers are to be enabled to support pupils in this way then they themselves need the support of organizations which are appropriately structured. We hope to contribute to the development of suitably responsive structures and practices through the chapters of this book.

It is perhaps surprising that relatively little has been written about learning difficulty in mathematics when comparison is made with learning difficulty in reading. Valuable contributions have been made by Denvir, Stolz and Brown (1982), Ahmed (1985, 1987) and Larcombe (1985) amongst others but recent changes require a new focus on many issues that confront teachers and schools today.

This book avoids the temptation of formulating a rigid set of directions for teacher action. The model of teacher action embedded in this book is that of the reflective practitioner (Schon, 1987) with ideas and suggestions to be used in what we regard as the only approach to the teaching of mathematics to children who experience difficulty in learning, that of an action/reflection problem solving cycle. We also start from the position which suggests that teaching and learning practices that are appropriate for children with SEN enrich schooling for all children. The practices generated by teachers who are actively involved in trying to make a creative response to children who are experiencing difficulty in learning are, in our view, those which will enhance the learning environment for all.

In Chapter 1 we have used the recent history of relevant legislation to construct an account of the strengths and limitations of current policy and special needs practices within mainstream schools. This is followed, in Chapter 2, by our interpretation of the movements within Mathematics Education that have led to the current aims and practices in classrooms today. We feel that teachers who are familiar with the current debates in the SEN field may wish to skip Chapter 1 and similarly mathematics teachers may wish to skip Chapter 2. Our intention in the remaining chapters has been to try to produce texts that are both amenable and of interest to both parties. In Chapter 3 we present an analysis of the way in which Psychology has influenced pedagogic developments within Mathematics Education. Our intention is to provide readers with a version of the psychological 'stories' that have formed the common sense of classroom practice. Chapter 4 then examines the classroom implications of the approaches that we consider to be of relevance to teachers working in secondary classrooms today. These practices rely heavily on an understanding of the ways in which pupils work in mathematics, the latter being the focus of Chapter 5. Throughout the book we focus on matters of assessment as it relates directly to teaching rather than as a mechanism for generating data which may be used in the process of comparing schools. We have opted to consider informal assessment rather than national and or normative procedures. In Chapter 6 we consider the communication issues that are raised within our analysis of responsive schooling in mathematics. Chapter 7 considers the question of whether it is appropriate and possible to identify a special pedagogy for those pupils who are seen to be special. Our final chapter presents a collection of thoughts on the matter of school organization. The emphasis here being on ways in which the organisation may be designed to respond to pedagogic needs rather than vice versa.

Acknowledgements

We would like to offer our grateful thanks to the unknown reviewer whose detailed comments and suggestions caused us to reflect on our efforts. We would also like to acknowledge the encouragement and forebearance of our families without whose support this volume would not have been possible.

—1—
Policy and practice in special needs

Our intention in this chapter is to provide a review of recent developments in special educational practice relating legislation to significant
developments in the classroom rather than a brief historical summary.
The framework of the changes in legislation is used to provide an
account of the conceptual shifts that have taken place in the context
of the ideological tensions which abound.

'The legislation governing special educational practice has a long
and convoluted history' (Galloway and Goodwin, 1987). In a sense,
legislation may be viewed as a relay of the contemporary ideological
positions on disability and educational difficulty. In this chapter we
will attempt to provide an overview of recent developments in order
that the possibilities for special needs services and curriculum reform
may be considered in the light of the social and educational forces
which have shaped current practices. Discussion will include the legislation, categorization and causation in relation to Special Educational
Needs as some of the background to current practice.

THE 1944 EDUCATION ACT

The 1944 Education Act introduced a legal framework and an
administrative system that associated categories of disability of mind
and body with forms of provision. Children were diagnosed, princi-
pally by medical authorities, as being members of particular disability
groups with which particular curriculum expectations and special
schools were associated. Special Education was viewed as being concerned with problems that existed mainly within the child and provision was organized in line with the classification of such children. The
practices of 'diagnosis' and the concept of 'disability' with which they
were linked were of medical origin. Eleven categories of handicap
were announced and it was the responsibility of the School Health
Service to carry out diagnoses. The categories were: deaf, partially
deaf, blind, partially sighted, physically handicapped, delicate,
diabetic, epileptic, educationally subnormal, speech deficient and

maladjusted. The 1944 Act also designated one group of children, those with a measured IQ below 50, as being outside the scope of education and it was not until 1970 that all children were considered as candidates for schooling (DES, 1970). Once referred to a special school, very few pupils returned to mainstream schools. Contact between teachers and pupils in special schools and their peers in mainstream schools was rare. Special schools invariably stood outside the mainstream systems of inspection, curriculum review, evaluation and advice. Teachers, pupils, and indeed their schools, were in a very real sense socially, locationally and functionally segregated.

The Warnock Report (DES, 1978) may be viewed as an expression of dissatisfaction with the existing legislation. It suggested a shift in the balance of power with respect to the definition of children's needs from Medicine to Education through Psychology. This was associated with a re-conceptualization of causation in terms of interactions between the strengths and weaknesses of the child and the positive and negative aspects of the environment rather than in terms of deficiencies within the child. Along with this concept of interactive causation came the understanding that it was not profitable to consider a fixed boundary between the SEN population and the 'normal' population. This period was marked by an increased awareness of the diversity of educational need within the 1944 Act categories and also by an increased understanding of the significant formative effects of social deprivation in early childhood. Classification of children's needs under the 1944 Act did not always achieve the most appropriate match in school provisions for those children involved. Norwich (1990a) summarizes the main arguments against the use of categories as follows:

1. children often suffer from more than one disability resulting in categorisation difficulties which affect school provision;
2. categories promote the idea that all children in the same category have similar educational needs;
3. categories as the basis for provision draw resources away from children not covered by the statutory categories;
4. categories have the effect of labelling children and schools adversely and this persists beyond school and can stigmatise unnecessarily. (p. 36)

He also discusses the beneficial effects of categories and in so doing highlights the extent to which confusion has arisen in the torrent of rhetoric associated with moves towards integration and the abandoning of categories. The model of causation which underpins much of the rhetoric Norwich discusses is relativist and interactionist. It is interactionist as special educational need is theorized in terms of interactions between 'within person' factors and environmental factors. It is relativist since need is thought to be relative to the context in which the person is placed. Norwich suggests that the supposed relativist interactionist perspective has in practice become narrowly environmentalist. His position is one which advances the argument for categories of resources and deficits in the process of decision making. Norwich argues that children should be thought of as individuals 'in the context of their educational progress, without prejudging the kind and location of provision to be made for them'.

The resolution of the tensions between those who would dispense with categories (e.g. Ainscow and Tweddle, 1988) and those such as Norwich (1990a) who see new uses for them may be far away. However, they may be seen to share assumptions which are of relevance to the present discussion.

> It is inappropriate and unproductive to:
> - exaggerate the differences between children with ordinary and exceptional needs;
> - treat all children who have a particular deficit as the same educationally;
> - segregate, distance and devalue children as persons merely on account of having deficit. (p. 41)

THE 1981 EDUCATION ACT

Goacher *et al.* in their report of research into procedures for assessing and making provision for children's special educational needs, commissioned by the Department of Education and Science, identified three main groupings of principles underlying the 1981 Act:

- principles concerned with the *nature* of special educational needs
- principles concerned with the *rights* of those with special educational needs (and their parents)
- principles concerned with the *effectiveness* of identifying, assessing and meeting special educational needs.

(from Goacher *et al.*, 1988)

These principles underpin the legislation and yet are in themselves laid open to actions designed to avoid their implementation. The clearest example of these 'somewhat ironic legislative quirks' relates to the intention that special educational provision should be made in ordinary schools. Local authorities were urged to make such provision and also furnished with conditions which have been interpreted as allowing them to simply maintain the *status quo*. Legislation stipulates that provision for individuals within a Local Education Authority (LEA) is dependent upon the following:

- his/her receiving the special educational provision he/she requires
- the provision of efficient education for the children with whom he/she will be educated
- the efficient use of resources.

Interestingly the 1993 Education Act contains similar clauses concerning the responsibilities of Health and Social Services in making special provision. Authorities were guided by the legislation within the following constraints:

- consider that the help requested 'is not necessary'
- (in the case of health authorities) 'having regard to the resources available to them . . . it is not reasonable to comply' or
- (in the case of social services) it conflicts with their 'statutory or other duties and obligations'.

The 1981 Education Act definition of special educational needs reflects contemporary views of the causes of educational difficulty. Section I of the Act relates a relativistic view of 'learning difficulty' to the need for special provision. Need is conceptualized in terms of provision that must be made if a child is to make educational progress 'a child has special educational needs if he has a learning difficulty which calls for special educational provision to be made for him' (p. 1). Critics have commented on the extent to which this new formulation of need allowed LEAs to continue to match needs with existing provision (Tomlinson, 1985), teachers to express their own needs and existing practices to remain unchanged or even expand (Tomlinson, 1985; Swann, 1985).

Individual needs are defined in terms of actions that are required in particular contexts and this tacitly announces the imperative of improving that provision, which counts as 'mainstream' or 'ordinary' in order to minimize the amount of perceived difficulty and consequent special need. Wedell (1990) notes that the 1981 Education Act has often been thought of as being concerned only with the procedures for drawing up legal 'statements' of need for about 2 per cent of the population rather than as introducing a broad view of need which extends to a much larger proportion whose needs may be met without recourse to a statement.

Certainly educational usage of concepts such as handicap and disability has given way to notions of educational difficulty and need. However some of these changes appear to be little more than name changes in practice. The two groups who constitute the majority of children in special schools are shown below in their respective forms.

FROM 1944 ACT Educationally Subnormal	TO 1981 ACT Moderate Learning Difficulty
Maladjusted	Emotional and Behavioural difficulty

Certainly the newer terms are less offensive but they are seen to function in much the same way as their predecessors. A teacher in a mainstream school today is quite likely to come across the following descriptors:

Mild Learning Difficulty (formerly Remedial)
Moderate Learning Difficulty   MLD
Emotional and Behavioural Difficulty   EBD
Specific Learning Difficulty (e.g. 'Dyslexia')   SpLD
Physical Disability or   PD
Physical and Neurological Impairment   PNI
Visual Impairment   VI
Hearing Impairment   HI

All these terms suffer from problems with definition and are often used in a confused and confusing manner.

AFTER THE 1981 ACT: INDIVIDUAL AND INSTITUTIONAL NEEDS

Associated with changes in terminology has been an increased acceptance that assessment must focus not only on individual difficulties but also on factors within schools which can prevent or exacerbate problems (NCC, 1989; ILEA, 1985; Galloway, 1985). This position was expressed in the Warnock Report's recommendation (DES, 1978) that teaching problems should, in the first stages, be the responsibility of those working in classrooms and schools. Goacher *et al.* (1988) suggest that local support arrangements are a significant factor associated with variations in the level of statutory assessment leading to Statements of SEN. This position is represented in the Education Act 1981 (section 2,5) which places a duty on governors to secure that headteachers and teachers identify and provide for children with SEN. Thus a major direction within SEN education has been improvement of the quality of educational provision in order to meet a broad range of educational need.

The period following the introduction of the 1981 Act witnessed the development of not only a new vocabulary but also new groupings of teachers working in and alongside mainstream schools. Many of the practices which have developed in response to the 1981 Act are based upon an assumption that co-operation will be most beneficial to the children involved. Awareness that as many as 20 per cent of the school population may have special needs at some time during their schooling carried with it implications for co-operation between teachers. It was always assumed that the majority of educational needs would be met by classroom teachers. The slogan became 'every teacher a teacher of special needs'. Intervention for the specialist teacher shifted from being exclusively focused on the child to being involved in some combination between the child and the teacher. Previously the remedial teacher had withdrawn children from ordinary lessons, now the support teacher worked alongside the classroom teacher in ordinary classrooms or offered advice outside teaching time.

Arguments in favour of this change where couched in terms of difficulties in transfer of training from withdrawal settings to mainstream settings and also restricted expectations of teachers and pupils in such settings. In the case of full-time special or remedial classes, concerns were raised about the narrowness of the curriculum just as they had been about separate special school classes.

When HMI (1989a) turned their attention to the *services* which were intended to support children in ordinary schools they found many causes for concern. They commented on the lack of explicit policy making with clear and co-ordinated leadership, the lack of time, resources and financial support made available and the inconsistency in provision across different LEAs. The survey of *pupils* with special educational needs in mainstream schools made the case that schools do need support. Again the inspectors found some signs of encouraging development but still noted that 75 per cent of schools used withdrawal of pupils with special educational needs in which the work was often unrelated to the classroom and less interesting and relevant than the missed classroom activity (HMI, 1989b). This resulted in pupils losing continuity with classroom work in both secondary and primary classes.

The move from patterns of full-time and part-time permanent or temporary withdrawal from mainstream classes towards greater support within the classroom was only successful when teachers collaborated in teaching, planning and reviewing lessons. In turn these acts of co-operation were invariably most successful in schools which had developed and maintained whole school policies on special educational needs.

The term 'support' became widely used and also developed many meanings. Support for teachers; support for schools; support for systems and support for children were all developed and often confused with one another.

THE 1988 EDUCATION ACT

The 1988 Education Act (DES, 1988) introduced an explicitly market-oriented framework into the state education system setting special needs within the organizational and financial framework of each individual school. This seems to stand in opposition to the commonly held belief that the diverse needs of Special Education can best be met through provision in which teachers and schools co-operate. Subsumed in the notion of support is the understanding that it is worthwhile and efficient to enable children to have access to whatever experiences are being provided within the school or within the local authority. In terms of the 1988 Act, where support was offered from outside the School either by specialist services or other schools, the question has now become one of who will pay for these forms of co-operation in the era of local financial management of schools. There is, therefore, an important question: 'can co-operative initiatives survive the pressure of market forces?'

The 1988 Act introduced a demand led, consumer-oriented system with a built-in financial incentives scheme. Money is made available to schools under the Local Management of Schools (LMS) scheme primarily on the basis of numbers of children enrolled at a school. Schools are being encouraged to market themselves in order to attract the highest numbers of pupils possible and thereby ensure economic security. Perhaps the most powerful indicator of school effectiveness available to these marketing exercises will be the eventual pattern of aggregated subject attainment scores, if these survive the ongoing review exercise.

Whilst common sense suggests that these indicators have, at minimum, to be balanced against the promotion of the school on other criteria, there remains the lingering fear that league tables of aggregated scores will serve to distort many aspects of schooling. Paragraph 81 of the report of the Elton Committee (DES, 1989a) provides a timely reminder that 'a school in which academic achievement is the only source of positive encouragement is likely to experience more difficulties with low achieving pupils'.

There are also a number of regulations which may effect the form of provision made for children with special needs inside mainstream schools. For example paragraph 36 of circular 6/89 allows children to be taught outside their Key Stage. If children are to be taught outside their expected Key Stage they would, in many cases, have to be placed in classes with children more than 2 years different from themselves. Research concerned to identify necessary conditions for successful integration suggests that children should never be placed in classes more than two years below their chronological age, schools may be tempted to recreate separate special classes for children taught outside their expected Key Stage. Informal arrangements such as this may be made without reference to outside agencies whereas formal disapplication or modification of the National Curriculum involves elaborate procedures and possible appeals.

In 1992 the Audit Commission and HMI report on the working of the 1981 Act entitled *Getting in on the Act* (HMI/Audit Commission, 1992) considered how effectively schools and LEAs were making provision for children with SEN. This report was published at a time when there was great concern that those charged with the responsibility of drafting new educational legislation had 'very limited understanding of developments and problems in the field' and 'that issues of SEN [were] well down on the government's list of priorities' (Mittler, 1992, p. 150).

Despite earlier concerns about the combined effects of open enrolment, between school competition and the publication of crude measures of school worth (Daniels and Ware, 1990) the report suggested that a greater proportion of pupils with SEN were being educated in mainstream schools and that the majority of headteachers did *not* show signs of increased unwillingness to accept such pupils. The report further suggested that the process of integration carried with it higher levels of expectation of pupils in schools where awareness of SEN had been increased. However, the report also identified serious deficiencies in provision. Vevers suggests that the substance of the 1981 Act, or any legislation which followed, would only be fully implemented if three key groupings of concern became the direct object of attention. The problems identified were:

1. Lack of clarity particularly with respect to the level of need that requires extra provision. As a consequence parents appear to be unclear as to their entitlements, schools are often unclear as to what their responsibilities are and LEAs have difficulty in managing limited resources in the context of vague commitments to locally defined groupings.
2. Lack of accountability in relations between LEAs, schools and parents. Parents rights appear to be extremely vulnerable to the vicissitudes of local systems of assessment and school placement. As a consequence parents often have to wait far too long for their children to be assessed and often have little chance to influence the decision as to which school their child will be placed in.
3. Lack of incentives for schools and LEAs to improve their work with pupils with SEN.

(from Vevers, 1992)

As judged by Wedell's (1993a) summary there are many causes for concern that may be seen to be taking their toll in schools. He notes the decrease in SEN staffing and the associated rise in the number of schools reporting concerns about the resource implication of SEN pupils. Patterns of provision are similarly undergoing a period of forced change. An increase in percentage of pupils with statements has been reported in Evans and Lunt (1992). An increase in numbers of pupils excluded has also been established (12.5 per cent of pupils excluded had statements) (DFE, 1992).

Findings from a report prepared by the Office for Standards in Education (OFSTED) entitled *Special Needs and the National Curriculum 1991–92: The Implementation of the Curricular Requirements of the Education Reform Act* points to five issues which will need to be tackled if progress within the National Curriculum is to continue for pupils with SEN:

1. Schools generally, and special schools in particular, should review and monitor their curriculum to assess how well it provides the access for pupils with special needs required by the 1988 Education Act.
2. As momentum seems to diminish over the course of the school year, lesson planning needs to focus more carefully upon the National Curriculum programmes of study and statements of attainment and assessments of pupils' performance needs to be taken into account when progression is being planned.
3. Assessment of educational performance is still a weak aspect of work in many schools and should be addressed more urgently in in-service training and arrangements for assessing, recording and reporting pupils' performance in order to match work successfully to ability and special needs.
4. Schools need to conduct a thorough audit of provision of books and teaching materials for pupils with special educational needs, and to improve it since, in a significant number of schools, inadequate provision presents obstacles to pupils' progress in some subjects; work could be more closely matched to pupils' abilities.
5. Additional support provided by a special support assistant is sometimes wasted whereas when it is planned and co-ordinated in ways that complement the work of the teacher, the benefits to the pupils can be enormous.

(from OFSTED, 1993a)

The report is based on a survey of 173 special schools, 38 primary schools and 50 secondary schools during the school year September 1991 to July 1992.

Other points that emerge from the report are that half of the primary schools surveyed had no written policy on special educational needs and while two thirds of secondary schools had a policy only half of them put the policy into practice (pp. 13–14). Although more than half the primary schools and almost all the secondary schools had a teacher designated as co-ordinator for special educational needs only half the primary school co-ordinators and around

60 per cent of the secondary school co-ordinators made a positive impact on provision and practice for pupils with special needs (pp. 12–13). These general findings about policy development and implementation are extended by the HMI survey of practices concerned with the integration of pupils with Moderate Learning Difficulties (MLD) into secondary schools (HMI, 1993). The MLD group comprise some 52 per cent of the special school population (HMI/Audit Commission, 1992). Along with pupils described as having Emotional and Behavioural Difficulties (EBD) they form the population most 'at risk' from variation in local policy and practice (OFSTED/Audit Commission, 1992).

HMI (1993) found relatively few examples of successful integration of pupils with MLD from special schools into secondary schools exist and argued that more pupils could cope with transfer. They suggested that there is too great an element of chance as to whether a pupil has the opportunity to be integrated from special school. From the examples of good practice they observed, they concluded that careful preparation for integration is crucial and that the benefits to pupils are largely social although the prospects of a broader curriculum is much valued by parents. Although Local Authorities did not hinder integration few were seen to be active in encouraging it. HMI voiced particular concerns about many arrangements in the teaching of mathematics. These will be explored in Chapters 4 and 5.

Thus it would seem that SEN policy and practice within secondary schools is struggling to realise the goals established in the rhetoric surrounding the Warnock Report and the implementation of the 1981 Act. Further disquieting information comes from an NUT survey of trends in Support Service provision:

- The number of LEAs cutting special education support service provision has increased. For 1993–94, the number of LEAs cutting particular services has escalated sharply.
- Funding for 'low incidence' support services, such as the visual and hearing impaired services, is being delegated in an increasing number of LEAs despite indications from the DFE that such services should be held centrally in both Circular 7/91 (DES, 1991) and in a subsequent consultative document (DFE, 1993) sent to chief education officers in the LEAs.
- An increasing number of LEAs are reducing provision in services such as educational psychology and education welfare, and visual impairment services, which the government deems essential, as well as in the wider range of SEN support services. In addition there is a small core of LEAs which have reduced consistently particular services over the three-year period.
- LEAs making cuts in services are not necessarily the same ones as

those delegating provision. However those LEAs delegating services which do not come within the LEA's own definition of *essential* services are very likely to cut those services' funding.

(from Bangs, 1993)

Thus there are very real concerns about the prospects for services which were originally designed to support individual children in schools and also to support the development of schools as service providers. One potential outcome of some of these trends is that the interactive aspect of the SEN concept will be lost in practices which attend to individuals in isolation as aspects of service delivery, institutional development and preventative work are neglected.

THE 1993 EDUCATION ACT AND THE CODE OF PRACTICE

In line with many of the changes being introduced in other areas of state services the HMI/Audit Commission report proposes that LEAs should act as clients purchasing SEN provision, on behalf of pupils, from schools and services. This suggestion is offered as a way of achieving the politically required delegation of resources and at the same time affording LEAs a new role as protector of SEN interests in the context of devolved finances.

The 1993 Act also introduces a new system of SEN tribunals and sets out their composition, duties and procedures. These independent tribunals may serve to correct the imbalances in legal power inherent in the 1981 Act appeals procedures. They may also come to consume large amounts of time and thus drain the limited resources available to finance SEN arrangements. The Association of Metropolitan Authorities make the following comment in relation to parents' rights:

> One underlying problem which has bedevilled SEN in the decade since implementation of the 1981 Act has been ... the availability of resources. Much of the dissatisfaction with special educational needs provision is caused by the difficult decisions occasioned by finite LEA resources. Improved rights of parental appeal will not, for example, improve provision, although one effect may be to sharpen the quality of decision making about the allocation of available resources.
>
> (from Association of Metropolitan Authorities, 1993)

Parents' rights have received further clarification in the 1993 Education Act, the provisions of which were explained by Baroness Blatch as reported in Hansard as follows:

> On the LEA there is ... 'A duty to integrate a child with a (SEN) statement ... into a mainstream school, provided certain reasonable conditions are met and, unless the parent wishes his child to attend a special school.' and further 'If the parent expresses a preference or makes representations for a special school placement, the LEA's duty to

integrate falls away, but the LEA's power to name a mainstream school does not . . .'.

(Hansard, 6 July 1993, Column 1261)

The Code of Practice on Special Educational Needs, announced in the 1993 Act, was circulated in draft form for wide-ranging consultation by the Department for Education (DFE) and issued in the final version during May 1994. The basic principles generating the Code remained intact and may be summarized as follows:

- Firstly, the needs of both the 2 per cent of children with statements and the 18 per cent without the statements of special educational needs should be identified and assessed as early and as quickly as possible.
- Secondly, provision for all children with special educational needs should be made by the 'most appropriate agency', usually the child's mainstream school, without a statutory assessment but, in a small number of cases, through the issue of a statement of SEN by the LEA.
- Thirdly, schools should receive clear guidance on the steps they should take to identify, assess and monitor all children with special educational needs.
- Fourthly, schools and LEAs should be given clear criteria as to when statutory assessment might be necessary and when a statement should follow; the criteria should generate greater objectivity and hence greater national consistency in the making of assessment and statements.
- Fifthly, LEAs should receive clear guidance on the procedures which they were to adopt in making assessments. These, together with the regulations, would subject LEAs to time limits; promote partnership between LEAs and parents throughout the assessment and state-menting processes; promote partnership between LEAs and schools, grant maintained and LEA maintained, mainstream and special; promote partnership between LEAs and other statutory agencies; acknowledge the important contribution which voluntary bodies were able to make to assessments; make provision for LEAs to take into account the ascertainable wishes and feelings of the child concerned, considered in the light of his or her age and understanding.
- Sixthly, the code and regulations should ensure that LEAs were given guidance in the writing of clear, thorough and specific statements and on the naming of an appropriate school in the light of parental preference or representations, whether the school was in the maintained, non-maintained or independent sector and whether it was day or residential.

(from Peter, 1993a)

The final version of the Code of Practice gives practical guidance to

LEAs and schools on how to meet their respective responsibilities for children with SEN. It is also anticipated that it will provide some form of 'common sense' of expectations of SEN practice which will lead to greater consistency across LEAs. The regulations, drafted along with the Code, are designed to ensure greater specificity in the writing of statements and conduct and participation in annual reviews of these statements. The Code is supplemented by guidance on: the organization of special schools; the issues to be addressed in school SEN policies; and the operation of the parental appeals tribunals established by the 1993 Act. In that the 1993 Act states that all those concerned with SEN practices must have 'regard' to the Code, OFSTED inspections will focus on its operation in practice.

Wedell (1993b) identified the three main aspects of the Code as being concerned with the ways schools come to meet SEN; the ways in which decisions come to be made; and the ways in which reviews are carried out. He asks whether these aspects of the Code will maintain the rights of participants; be effective in promoting the meeting of SEN in integrated settings; and promote the efficient use of resources.

In that the Code uses, and to some extent develops, the five stages of assessment and intervention proposed by the Warnock Report, these questions may be considered through reference to the new structure. The first three stages are school based and are thus the ones that are of concern here. Stage One primarily involves the classroom teacher who registers concern about a pupil's performance in school and may seek advice and support from the Special Educational Needs Co-ordinator (SENCO). They will gather relevant information about the pupil from the school, the parent and (at last!) the child. On the basis of this information a decision is made as to whether information should be sought from Health and Social Services. All this action requires time. Partly there is a need for time to gather and collate information. Above all there is a need for time to think about the concerns that are held by the classroom teacher. The teaching problems that pupils present teachers are by their definition rarely open to simple solutions. Classroom teachers are faced with an increasing array of demands, many of which are generated by the system of market forces in which schooling is now placed. Their ability to cope with the 'normal' demands of classroom and school life is under considerable pressure. One, all too familiar, way of making life tolerable again is to construct a description of the pupil's needs which meets the specification of provision that is known to exist. If this practice of 'slipping' pupils who cause concern into whatever provision happens to be available is to be avoided there is a need for classroom teachers and SENCOs to have time to plan and consult. They also need to be appropriately trained. The demise of 'earmarked' funding for SENCO training is one cause for concern. The likelihood of the new format of initial teacher training providing the necessary preparation in SEN work for classroom teachers is another. The prospect of an increase in the numbers of untrained SENCOs in mainstream secondary schools who may well have a number of additional responsibilities generated by the demands of the National Curriculum would appear to be very real in the context of what may prove to be diminishing resources for Additional Educational Needs.

At Stage Two of the process the SENCO takes the lead in assessing the pupil's difficulty, and also takes 'prime responsibility for managing the child's special educational provision'. At Stage Three the school may decide to call upon external specialist support. However, the extent to which LEAs will be able to plan and maintain cost effective and sufficiently flexible forms of support service is under question as noted above. In that external specialist support is only mentioned at Stage Three there would appear to be little chance of the preventative work developed by SEN support services in the wake of the implementation of the 1981 Act finding a 'place of safety' within the Code.

Peter (1993b) questioned the way in which these procedures would impact on the diversity of schools:

> Will 'better' schools be better at working the Code and thus be better at getting resources?

If an interactional concept of the causation of SEN is applied it would follow that a school which was experiencing and struggling with general managerial and pedagogic difficulties would be likely to have more pupils who should 'register concern' than a school that was in a more equable position. It remains to be seen whether the Code will seek to disadvantage some schools by virtue of its managerial demands.

Overall the Code of Practice contains much that may be regarded as positive and is to be welcomed. It does go some way to establishing a 'level playing field' for the implementation by virtue of the new, more specific, procedures. It also provides a move towards clarity in the specification of the respective roles of schools, parents and LEAs. However, there remains the question as to whether the changes introduced in the 1993 Education Act will be fully implemented. A rereading of the DES commissioned study by Goacher *et al.* (1988) of the implementation of the 1981 Act suggests that a subtle process of interpretation and minimal compliance may result. The question as to whether the Code serves to focus attention on the individual in isolation rather than the individual in a curriculum, classroom and school social context remains open. If the National Curriculum exercise, with its associated market-oriented machinery, serves to reduce the possibility of making 'schooling more responsive to all', as it may, then accounts of individual difficulty may revert to the discourse of deficiency.

A EUROPEAN PERSPECTIVE

It is perhaps worth supplementing these comments on the situation in the UK with a few observations from a broader European perspective. The European Integration Network (EIN) is a multi-disciplinary exchange and research programme involving communities in Denmark, Germany, Italy, Spain and the United Kingdom. The major focus of the programme has been on the integration of children with special educational needs into mainstream settings in schools and communities with a specific reference to decision making processes. The point at which extra resources are given by the state and its agencies to an individual in need provides the unifying inter-cultural point of common concern. Local cultures, including legislative and social imperatives, and their implications for research activity are discussed. Common themes in the transition and transformation of the various forms of welfare state provision within the member countries are identified and analysed.

The most important overall trend observed is, not surprisingly, from the rhetoric of segregation to the rhetoric of integration. The reality involves a movement from provision in which individuals become dependent to that in which there is a level of independence, autonomy and empowerment. The position of the child as an active agent in decision making about provision and perhaps more importantly as an active participant in the teaching and learning process will be discussed in Chapter 3. A significant trend associated with these notions has been the move towards a concern for the quality of life rather than mere access to services.

Thus a European perspective on the teaching of mathematics to children with SEN in mainstream secondary schools might cause us to reflect on the dynamics of teaching and learning relationships and their consequences cast in terms of independent and autonomous learner behaviour and its consequences for quality of life. These themes will be explored through the main body of the rest of the book.

If the pattern of provision that has emerged following the implementation of the 1981 and 1988 Acts tells us anything it is that we have no clear and convincing way of distinguishing between those who need special resources and those who do not. The boundary between these two groups reflects local priorities and perspectives rather than the implementation of objective criteria. Whatever the future holds for the definition of this boundary we will be discussing the mathematical prospects for a broad range of children in terms which at one time are of relevance to all children and at another are referenced to restricted groups defined in terms of specific learner characteristics.

SUMMARY

The SEN field prior to the 1981 Act was influenced by categories of within person deficits. Categories had been associated with provisions (e.g. special schools) and interventions (e.g. special pedagogies or curricula). Once assigned to a category pupils tended to be treated in terms of the needs associated with the category rather than their own individual needs.

The 1981 Act promoted the view that individual SEN arise from the *interaction* of individual and environmental factors. Individual needs were thought to be relative to specific provisions and particular circumstances. A procedure for identifying individual needs was developed although, in practice, this proved to be cumbersome and not always impartial despite the articulation of parental rights.

The 1988 Act brought notions of the 'market' to the world of education. As the currency of this new market was founded on aggregated attainment scores concerns were raised for the position of pupils whose attainments were seen to be harmful to overall school profiles. It did create the opportunity for schools to make their own decisions about priority needs of the school.

The 1993 Act and its associated profusion of circulars has introduced a relatively high degree of specificity to the general understanding of individual consumer rights and professional and institutional responsibilities. In so doing it may afford pupils with SEN some protection from an unfettered market. Without some degree of caution, it may lead to the retrograde step of there being an undue focus of attention on individuals rather than individuals in contexts.

European initiatives in education may cause us to reflect as to whether principles of 'access' and 'entitlement' are sufficient without the development of an operational notion of 'quality of life' for those with SEN in mainstream and special settings.

Change and challenge in mathematics teaching

In the previous chapter, we considered developments in the legislation affecting the teaching of pupils with special educational needs that have led to the present position with many such pupils integrated into the mainstream school. This chapter reviews changes in the content and teaching approaches in secondary mathematics that have taken place independently but parallel to those above. Since the 1960s there have been many changes in the mathematics curriculum for secondary schools and many changes in teaching methodology. We will attempt to give reasons for some of these changes, to show how the aims of mathematics teaching have been modified and outline the present position since the introduction of the National Curriculum. School mathematics has evolved to reflect not only the needs of society but also changes in the subject matter most relevant to higher mathematics. We will discuss the introduction of 'Modern Mathematics' and changes in teaching approaches developed as new paradigms for learning have been proposed by psychologists including Piaget, Bruner, Dienes and others. We will discuss the influences of the Cockcroft Report (1982) and the introduction of the National Curriculum (1988, 1991, 1994) and changes in assessment procedures and the examination system.

INFLUENCES FOR CHANGE IN SECONDARY SCHOOL MATHEMATICS

The influence of learning paradigms

Curriculum changes in school mathematics have resulted from new and modified theories of learning (e.g. Piaget 1952; Dienes 1960; Bruner 1966) and have more recently been guided by reports like that of the Report of the Cockcroft Committee of Inquiry into the Teaching of Mathematics in Schools, *Mathematics Counts* (DES, 1982) and by legislation (Education Reform Act, 1988). This section will briefly introduce considerations relating to learning theories which will be developed more fully later in the book.

The 'transmission' model for learning in which knowledge is passed from the knower (teacher) and passively received by the learner has been replaced by the 'constructivist' paradigm for learning in which learners are actively involved in constructing their own knowledge. The move away from a transmission approach of rote learning through 'drill and practice' reflects better understanding of how mathematics is successfully learned through interactions in which learners participate in the construction of their own knowledge rather than 'receiving' facts and information to be remembered. As well as addressing the changing needs of society where there is need for confident, independent thinking in mathematics, this increased emphasis on the construction and communication of mathematics is fundamental to the *constructivist* paradigm for learning. Constructivism acknowledges a sharp distinction between teaching, where the aim is to generate understanding in the pupil, and training, where the purpose is to generate repetitive behaviour. Jaworski (1988) presents an interesting discussion of the way a constructivist perspective relates to some of the issues in mathematics teaching today, but every experienced teacher is aware of the way pupils' interpretations do not always conform with more standard meanings. When working with pupils on mathematical tasks, teachers will often find that pupils construct their own procedures rather than using taught methods. These methods may be naive e.g. counting on fingers instead of using a multiplication fact, but reflect the child's understanding of the task and their confidence with different procedures. This book proposes ways in which learning may be developed from the child's own framework of understanding to improve confidence rather than imposing methodologies that will erode confidence and inhibit independent thinking.

'Modern mathematics': Pre-Cockcroft

As well as developments in the theories of children's learning in mathematics, changes in school have been influenced by trends in university mathematics and a move to meet the needs of a changing society. Such changes in mathematics teaching are difficult to analyse by all but those most closely associated with their design and implementation. But the spread of 'modern mathematics' and the 'back to basics' movement have generated emotional reactions from a population whose experiences 'qualify' them to speak knowledgeably from their sometimes narrow personal perspectives. Change from the mathematics valued in Victorian times, such as the four rules of arithmetic, has been most notable from the middle of this century and currently revolves around the implementation of a National Curriculum which will take us into the twenty-first century.

Discussions signalling the need for change in school mathematics are considered in detail in Cooper (1985) *Renegotiating Secondary School Mathematics*, which documents conferences and meetings between mathematicians in universities, schools, business and industry to determine appropriate adaptations of the school curriculum. Modern mathematics began to appear widely in the early 1960s with a number of projects (see Mathematical Association Pamphlet, *Mathematics Projects in British Secondary Schools*, 1968a) proposing changes in secondary mathematics in part to reflect mathematical interests within the universities and also to encompass a changing perspective of the purposes of teaching mathematics. New syllabuses incorporated not only a change in content with, for example, the introduction of 'modern algebra', but also considered approaches that began to emphasize understanding and applications to 'real-life' problems. Topics like sets and logic, studied by university mathematicians in their exploration of the 'foundations of mathematics' found a place in lower school mathematics often to the dismay of 'traditional' teachers who could be faced with rapidly changing syllabuses without adequate access to the justifications for such change.

Most significant was the recognition of mathematics as a process, a way of thinking and working, as well as a body of facts and skills to be acquired. With the shift away from 'drill and practice' the phrase 'discovery learning' signalled an approach to mathematics teaching that incorporated practical activity and involvement of the children in their own learning. Considerable enthusiasm developed among mathematics teachers as they broadened the scope of mathematics teaching to include applications relevant to the pupils own experiences and used activities and examples to make mathematics more accessible to pupils of all abilities.

The Mathematical Association published a report *Mathematics Eleven to Sixteen* (1974) in which it proposed 'to take stock of what is going on, to pull together the significant threads in school mathematics today and to weave them into a coherent whole'. The report did not attempt 'to provide detailed syllabuses for the rapidly changing conditions of the present time' but to provide a 'background against which they [mathematics teachers] can develop their own courses'. For this was a time in which teachers were centrally involved in decisions about course content as well as teaching approaches and assessment procedures:

Considerable developments have ... been taking place in secondary schools themselves. In many areas these changes have been accelerated not only by significant projects and experiments in mathematics teaching, but also by the differing modes of CSE examination, with their declared aim of trying to reflect and encourage the best of mathematics learning. In a rapidly changing technological society the primary aim is progressively that of nurturing so far as is possible pupils' ability to think clearly and work effectively in a mathematical situation, to make judgements and discriminate, and to apply the concepts and skills which they have developed, rather than to perform techniques as ends in themselves and largely in isolation from the real world – an emphasis on 'know-how' rather than on knowledge. (p. 174)

As practical activity was advocated within the changing environment for mathematics teaching, mathematics laboratories were introduced into many schools (see the Mathematical Association Report, *Mathematics Laboratories in Schools*, 1968b) and resources for practical mathematics were enhanced. Investment in material resources has seen a decline in more recent years reflecting the economic climate in schools, but a majority (two-thirds) of schools retain 'a range of equipment and resources available for teaching mathematics which is at least satisfactory' (OFSTED, 1993b).

The Cockcroft Report

Publication of the Report of the Committee of Enquiry into the Teaching of Mathematics, *Mathematics Counts* (DES, 1982) led to further re-evaluation of many aspects of teaching mathematics including teaching approaches and issues of attitude and confidence among pupils. Recognition of the need for a variety of teaching approaches came in the now celebrated paragraph 243:

Mathematics teaching at all levels should include opportunities for:

- exposition by the teacher;
- discussion between teacher and pupils and between pupils themselves;
- appropriate practical work;
- consolidation and practice of fundamental skills and routines;
- problem solving, including the application of mathematics to everyday situations;
- investigational work.

This specific reference to the need for a variety of teaching styles has led to substantial reviews of the aims in mathematics teaching and to the introduction of investigations and open-ended tasks incorporating discussion and collaborative work. The report also stressed that attention should be paid to developing in pupils a positive attitude towards mathematics and identified the necessity for a broad curriculum for all pupils including 'pupils whose attainment is very low' with adequate emphasis on oral work. Publication of a foundation list of mathematical topics, together with this re-appraisal of mathematics teaching, its aims and methodology, led the way to further developments in mathematics teaching and changes in the examination system with expansion to include the majority of secondary school pupils.

EXAMINATIONS

With the raising of the school leaving age to sixteen in the 1970s, the CSE examination had been introduced to provide a qualification for some of the pupils unable to achieve success in the traditional O-level examinations and to reflect the changing emphasis of school mathematics. Since O-level was targeted at a very small proportion of the population (about the top 20 per cent) and resulted in failure for approximately one-third of entrants, this was a welcome innovation but did not extend to involve the majority of pupils with SEN. Inadequacies of the O-level and CSE systems of examination at sixteen are discussed in Isaacson (1987) when outlining the introduction of GCSE as a common examination for the majority of pupils at the end of compulsory schooling:

> One of the worst aspects of O level and CSE mathematics has been that conscientious mathematics teachers were forced into spending a lot of their time and energy (and that of their pupils) teaching how to pass the mathematics examinations, instead of being able to concentrate on creating good conditions for learning mathematics. Syllabuses have been too large, often idiosyncratic, and with content which was conceptually beyond many of the pupils for whom it was intended. (p. 5)

There was a feeling that pupils were being exposed for what they did not know or could not do, rather than being given an opportunity to demonstrate what they could achieve. Many young people were leaving school at sixteen without confidence to tackle mathematics problems and with a deeply rooted anxiety about mathematics. Under such conditions it was inappropriate to subject low-attainers to formal examination procedures from which they had no hope of gaining any qualification.

Introduction of the GCSE as a common examination at sixteen, not only removed anomalies inherent in the system of two parallel examinations aimed at the same population but marked a shift away from norm-referenced assessment where a percentage of the entrants were intended to fail, to a criterion-referenced procedure (Isaacson, 1987). The hallmark of the new examination was essentially the introduction of a positive approach enabling credit to be given to individuals' achievements at a variety of levels to reflect the differing population of examination entrants. Initially, GCSE was targeted at the same 60 per cent of the population as O-level and CSE taken together, but with an opportunity that 'in the proposed new grading system, if standards of achievement rise, a greater proportion of the population may achieve GCSE passes' (ibid, p. 9). As assessment procedures extended to incorporate continuous assessment and course work, conditions became more favourable for extending entries to those pupils of low ability previously outside the scope of public examinations in mathematics (though arithmetic examinations had been offered as a possible, if not wholly desirable alternative). Course work was seen to provide a means by which positive achievements could be accumulated over a period of time by all pupils though its effects were not uniform across gender and social class.

In the GCSE, grades were related to criteria and some graded assessment schemes were introduced that were particularly designed to meet the needs of the lower-attainment levels (i.e. the 40 per cent of the school leaving population for whom GCSE initially was not intended). Isaacson (1987) lists such examples and describes in more detail the GAIM project (1988) based on research into grade related criteria for GCSE and aimed at providing a 'detailed cumulative record of a student's attainment in mathematics' for all eleven- to sixteen-year-olds in comprehensive schools. The success of such projects extended the population of school leavers with a qualification and enhanced confidence in mathematics.

Introduction of the National Curriculum

The most significant recent change in school mathematics has been the introduction of a National Curriculum that identifies Programmes of Study at ten different levels to be the basis of study for all secondary school pupils including those with SEN. Teacher assessment is intended to identify the level of study for each pupil and teachers then provide an appropriate programme matched to the needs of individuals. Discussion of the implications of current legislation will be found throughout this book but this chapter will first reflect the nature of changes in school mathematics that are resulting from the publication of the National Curriculum in Mathematics (1991).

Current legislation places increased emphasis on the *processes* of mathematics which now form the basis for the first of four Attainment Targets. This Attainment Target involves the processes of 'Using and Applying Mathematics' and may be related to three strands:

(i) *applications*: developing problem solving strategies including formulating questions and investigating problem situations, pursuing open-ended tasks and applying mathematics to 'real world' problems;

(ii) *communicating*: discussing, interpreting and reporting in verbal as well as diagrammatic and symbolic formats;

(iii) *reasoning*: developing ideas of logical argument, justifying findings and results, generalizing and proving.

This area of study does not identify any specific content but requires a teaching and learning approach in which the uses and applications of mathematics permeate and influence all work in mathematics. At the time of going to press, there is some question of whether 'Using and Applying' could be integrated into other Attainment Targets rather than constituting a separate Attainment Target for explicit assessment. We hope that this will not happen as many positive changes in school have resulted from teachers focusing on the processes of mathematics, their recording and applications to problems. Difficulties planning for and assessing such work presents challenges to teachers but does address the fundamental question of what mathematical thinking and communication are all about.

The National Curriculum Council (INSET Resources) booklet (1992) *Using and Applying Mathematics: Notes for Teachers at Key Stages 1–4* helps teachers understand the structure and demands of this area of mathematics teaching and consider appropriate activities. This booklet suggests ways that using and applying is **integral** to the learning of mathematics and needs to be 'built-in' rather than 'bolt-on'. Not only should the aim be to develop problem solving and investigational strategies but also to develop the pupil's ability to apply mathematics to a range of contexts. Development of a positive attitude to mathematics, identified within the Cockcroft Report to be a crucial element in mathematics learning, may be established where problems relate to pupils experiences and a sense of ownership is developed.

Through collaborative work and discussion, pupils may be helped to develop a range of personal qualities and develop a sense of what mathematics is about. Clearly the aims of such teaching must be understood and agreed by both mathematics and support teachers whose understanding of mathematics teaching may be based on little more than personal experience. Fundamental to this approach is the understanding that mathematics should develop in pupils a way of thinking that explains patterns rather than a collection of often unrelated facts. To bring SEN pupils to an understanding of the relationships and patterns that constitute mathematics itself, they will need to be involved with practical tasks, *applying* mathematics to 'real-life' problems, exploring and investigating their findings and discussing their thinking with peers and teachers.

IMPLEMENTING MATHEMATICS AS A PROCESS

Mathematics may be used as a powerful tool to make sense of the real world or to engage in the creative activity of exploring and explaining patterns and relationships. This is often achieved through investigative approaches to learning. This does not refer to the 'investigations once a week' approach that has been adopted by some schools, but a more open-ended approach to tasks that may engage the pupils in an element of creativity. A useful discussion and examples are given in the Non-Statutory Guidance to the National Curriculum including suggestions to modify tasks like '3 × 5 = ' and offer the alternative 'Make up some questions whose answer is 15' or 'What do we call a five-sided shape' replaced by 'What shapes/configurations can you make with five lines?'

Some teachers seem to believe that pupils with SEN are not capable of investigational work, but research projects like the Low Attainers in Mathematics Project (LAMP) and the Raising Achievements in Mathematics Project (RAMP) report that low-attaining pupils involved in this sort of teaching approach 'thrive on a kind of learning which requires a minimum of factual knowledge, a large element of challenge and a great deal of experience in dealing with situations using particular kinds of thinking and practical skills' (Trickett and Sulke, 1988, p. 110). The scope for discussion and much wider consideration of related ideas soon becomes clear and pupils develop 'ownership' of the mathematics with which they are involved. As well as this increased potential for knowledge learning, pupils may enjoy the autonomy and scope for creativity, be encouraged in their mathematical thinking and, as a consequence, develop a more positive attitude to the subject generally.

Many pupils with SEN will experience difficulty structuring their own thinking and finding language appropriate to discuss their ideas. This can inhibit learning unless planning takes account of these difficulties. In their discussion document *Mathematics from 5 to 16* (HMI, 1985) HMI suggest that 'practical work [can] enhance problem solving and investigations by making the tasks more accessible in the initial stages and increasing awareness and interest among pupils'. Through practical activities, pupils may begin to talk about actual experiences and observations from which they may later abstract mathematical meanings. This document goes on to point out that 'without sufficient practical experiences the pupils are unable to relate abstract mathematical concepts to any form of reality. *All pupils benefit from appropriate practical work* ... whatever their age or ability' (p. 39).

Such recommendations appear to have made some impact on classroom practice. In the main findings of a Report by HMI *The*

Implementation of the Curricular Requirements of the Education Reform Act: Mathematics – Key Stages 1 and 3 the First Year 1989–90 (HMI, 1991) it is stated that, 'Pupils learned more effectively when they were provided with a variety of learning materials and experiences such as practical work, problem solving and discussion' but 'the level of resources for practical work in year 7 . . . was unsatisfactory largely because mathematics was not regarded by the department or school as a practical subject.'

In the more recent report *The Implementation of the Curricular Requirements of the Education Reform Act: Mathematics – Key Stages 1, 2, 3 and 4, the Fourth Year 1992–93* (OFSTED, 1993b) Her Majesty's Chief Inspector reports that:

> the range of equipment and resources available for teaching mathematics was at least satisfactory in just over two-thirds of the schools; it was good or very good in a quarter. Schools with good provision had a range of equipment, including construction kits and routine apparatus, which was particularly well used in Key Stage 3 to support mathematical learning and to promote the formation and development of concepts.

The fundamental aim in mathematics teaching is to equip pupils with the strategies, skills and knowledge and perhaps above all the confidence to *use* their mathematics to solve problems they will undoubtedly meet throughout their lives. Problem solving requires a large variety of skills including interpreting information that is available, planning and working methodically, selecting appropriate resources and mathematics, checking results and trying alternative strategies, presenting results in a way that makes sense to other people, many of which do not come easily to pupils with learning difficulties. But if mathematics teaching does not provide individuals with skills to tackle the problems of 'real-life' an integral part of their preparation for life is missing. Further discussion of problem solving will follow in Chapters 4 and 6.

CURRICULUM CONTENT

As well as the focus on the processes involved in 'Using and Applying' mathematics which constitute the first Attainment Target of the National Curriculum, the content prescribed for mathematics divides the curriculum into three major areas of work each identified within the remaining Attainment Targets:

(ii) *number and algebra* in which number understanding is emphasized and skills include estimating results of calculations and interpreting solutions and algebra is developed through pattern

recognition and descriptions in verbal, diagrammatic and symbolic forms as well as using variables to express relationships;
(iii) *shape, space and measures*: developing spatial sense and understanding geometric relationships through using and moving shapes and establishing skills in measuring including estimation and accuracy skills;
(iv) *data handling* involving pupils in the collection and organization of data and in the exploration of probability and chance.

In each of these areas the Attainment Targets at ten progressive levels of achievement are linked with specific Programmes of Study that form the basis for assessment. Level Descriptors provide a statement that typifies the stage of mathematical attainment identified for each level from one to ten.

Particular problems may be associated with planning for special needs pupils who do not comfortably fit into any specific level of attainment or for whom progression through levels is an inappropriate perception for learning. Although a hierarchy for learning is implicit in all the documentation, research has shown (Denvir, 1986) that the outcome of teaching may not be predicted and certainly does not fit comfortably the pattern of a hierarchy of increasing complexity in skills and knowledge to be mastered.

Undue focus on the specific statements that identify assessment criteria will distort the curriculum and result in narrow and inadequate preparation for teaching. Support for planning must be sought in the Programmes of Study that are identified and also in the strands that identify the nature of different components and which can be found on a chart in documentation accompanying the Statutory Orders of the National Curriculum (1991).

Shape and Space, for example, may be usefully subdivided into four strands: shape, location, movement and measures, that encompass different attributes of shapes and suggest varying procedures for exploring relationships. As well as a clear focus on different properties of shapes, their movement and location, the terms 'using' and 'understanding' repeatedly indicate the importance in developing conceptual understanding alongside procedural skills. Special needs pupils will need the support of an approach that involves practical tasks and discussion to relate the characteristics of shapes to their movement and their uses. Personal experiences both within and outside the classroom can be connected in a way that was not possible when Euclidean geometry was the exclusive content of geometry lessons.

The Statutory Orders do not provide a comprehensive development in all aspects of mathematics that must be addressed nor do they identify the appropriate stages of development at which certain aspects may be introduced. The teaching of time, for example, receives scant recognition and is not associated with any particular level or programme of study in Key Stage 3 or 4. Although the specified content will help identify components of mathematics to be taught to pupils with SEN it does not provide a comprehensive preparation in mathematics and appropriate teaching programmes must be planned by teachers working together in schools. Successful planning is already evident in many schools but HMCI (OFSTED, 1993b) reports problems where too much reliance is placed on commercial schemes:

> An increasing number of the schools have restructured their course on a modular basis linked to each Attainment Target. The teachers who had begun to use this approach saw it as an effective means of managing the curriculum and its assessment. Much of this modification was based on existing commercial schemes. In some schools this led to an over-reliance by teachers on the publishers to implement changes in the mathematics curriculum. (p. 16)

The Non-Statutory Guidance (DES, 1989b) is a valuable source of help for teachers in their task of interpreting and implementing the Statutory Orders and sections addressing planning, progression and continuity are helpful. There is, however, acknowledgement that 'special educational needs' require specific guidance that will be available 'at a later date'. The Dearing Report (Dearing, 1993) acknowledges that little progress has been made in this direction and reaffirms the centrality of teacher action in the curriculum planning process:

> The majority of teachers of pupils with SEN do not want a complex and statutorily prescribed curriculum catering for every conceivable SEN. A slimmer statutory National Curriculum will, by providing time for use at the teacher's discretion, go a long way towards giving teachers the scope necessary to provide all pupils with a meaningful entitlement to a broad, balanced and relevant curriculum. There are, however, specific steps which need to be taken in order to ensure that the National Curriculum is an entitlement for all pupils. (p. 53)

Concern will inevitably arise from the requirement of Standard Assessment Tests (SATs) to be taken under examination conditions and restrictions on the amount of course work that may be presented for examination. This will affect low-attainers who may not achieve their potential with more formal pen and paper tests and for whom course work has been the most appropriate means of presenting evidence of attainment. The Dearing Report decouples the ten level attainment scale from the GCSE assessment exercise within Key Stage 4. It also announces the need to develop new ways of assessing low-attaining pupils particularly in the fourteen to sixteen age range: 'I recommend that the assessment and recording of achievement by pupils with SEN should be reviewed. The Schools Curriculum and

Assessment Authority (SCAA) should investigate ways in which the small steps of progress that pupils with SEN make are assessed, recorded and reported positively.' The Report also recognizes and emphasizes the valuable role played by teacher assessment: 'The recommendations in this Report for enhancing the status and effectiveness of teacher assessment will go some considerable way towards gaining wider acceptance of this as the main means of recognising the achievements of pupils with SEN.' Our emphasis throughout this book will accordingly be on informal methods of teacher assessment as an integral part of the teaching process.

MATHEMATICS FOR THE TWENTY-FIRST CENTURY

So how has the experience of learning mathematics changed from that familiar to older generations? For many generations school mathematics was taught as a mental discipline involving indisputable facts and standard procedures that were learned for their use and application in a non-technological society or for the aesthetic value and beauty of the subject. Phrases like the 'four rules of arithmetic' and 'geometry theorems', that may still be familiar to many parents and grandparents, indicate the formality that existed in mathematics teaching for all ages and all abilities. In Victorian times and well into this century society depended on human calculators trained to use standard procedures, learned in school and implemented in the workplace. Each individual took on trust the accounting of other persons or relied on using the standard procedures learned in childhood. The scope of mathematics teaching did not often extend beyond arithmetic lessons but, where it did so, the academic traditions of disciplines like Euclidean geometry were adhered to and mathematics lessons provided one of the most formal (and sometimes formidable) aspects of schooling.

The fundamental nature of mathematics has not altered but the widespread availability of modern technology has modified the expectations of school qualifications resulting in changed demands in mathematics being made upon mathematicians and upon individual members of society. Most important calculations are now undertaken by machines and computers are being further developed for design and control, to support and replace their human counterparts. This accounts for the current emphasis on understanding and developing 'number sense' rather than extended practice on standard written methods. Human involvement in calculating will continue to be crucial but routine procedures must give way to an emphasis on independent thinking and sound understanding of the principles underlying mathematical relationships. Collaboration and communication are acknowledged to be crucial for much of the problem solving that is undertaken in society today.

These changes have substantial implications for pupils learning school mathematics which must now address the role that mathematics will play in future society and the mathematics learning that will be fundamental in the home and in the workplace of tomorrow. What is clear is that individuals' thinking skills and their access to mathematical results must not be inhibited by the technology that society has come to depend upon. In arithmetic, for example, it is clear that routine procedures in the manipulation of numbers are no longer adequate skills. Calculators and computers are available to support learning and pupils now have access to enhanced problem solving procedures. Focus has shifted to emphasize conceptual understanding so that pupils may understand why procedures work and may develop their own methods in problem solving. Changes in the content of mathematics teaching relate not only to the powerful technical support available in the classroom but also to an assumption that the home and workplace are fundamentally changed from that of previous generations. Machinery is becoming more sophisticated, for example, microwave ovens and programmable video recorders involve mathematical procedures that should be accessible to all members of society.

Not only in mathematics but across the curriculum in English, history, geography and other subjects, computers can support pupils' organizational and planning skills and give them access to an exciting learning environment as well as developing competencies with technology that will support their learning and improve their opportunities for employment. The logical thinking and structured planning associated with mathematics learning now find applications more widely than ever before and mathematics is designated as a *core* subject for all pupils five to sixteen alongside English and Science.

AIMS IN MATHEMATICS TEACHING

As well as developing knowledge, skills and understanding within mathematics itself, there are broader aims in the education of pupils that have particular significance for special needs pupils. Mathematics is an essential means of *communication* through the interpretation of information involving mathematical elements, to the manipulation of symbols and data in a meaningful way. Mathematics can be used to describe, to explain, to illustrate and to predict. Newspapers, politicians, advertisers and retailers all use mathematical illustrations and data to influence individuals in society and some awareness of meanings is essential for all roles in society today.

HMI identify several additional aims of mathematics teaching in the booklet *Mathematics from 5 to 16*:

- *to encourage the effective use of mathematics as a tool* in a wide range of activities within both school and adult life: including activities ranging from designing in art and modelling in craft to planning a holiday or the construction of a motorway;
- *to develop appreciation of the relationships within mathematics* so that pupils may come to know that mathematics is not an arbitrary collection of disconnected items but has a coherent structure in which the various parts are inter-related;
- *to show mathematics as a process, as a creative activity* encouraging imagination, initiative and flexibility of mind;
- *to help pupils work in a systematic way* using logical strategies in a routine task or developing procedures for more complex challenges;
- *to encourage independence* so that pupils will ask and answer their own questions;
- *to provide opportunities for working co-operatively* within a group or team developing skills that are transferable in the school curriculum and sound preparation for life;
- *to develop pupils' confidence in their own abilities* providing both a challenge and a sense of achievement for all pupils.

(from HMI, 1985)

These all influence approaches to the teaching and learning of mathematics and decisions will need to take into account the aims and objectives in mathematics lessons, as well as the needs of the pupils.

Mathematics and the individual

For learners with SEN there are benefits and drawbacks in the changes that are being implemented in the mathematics curriculum in schools and the expectations associated with the National Curriculum. Independent thinking can be harnessed to address mathematical problems across a broad range of topics and not restricted to number problems. Limited skills can be drawn together to make connections that will enable pupils to establish a framework for understanding, with pupils discussing their ideas and listening to others. Pupils may no longer be regarded as passive recipients in the learning process and should be actively involved, both physically and mentally, if they are to be successful at learning mathematics in schools today. From the teacher's perspective, it is no longer adequate to teach isolated procedures that are rehearsed and reinforced through routine practice. Planning for effective teaching can not only address the breadth of curriculum content in mathematics but also the rich variations in strategies that will emerge as pupils propose their individual solution strategies to problems.

This may present a particular challenge to teachers of pupils with special needs where behavioural difficulties and classroom control may be fundamental issues that need to be addressed alongside changes in teaching approaches to mathematics. The opportunity to respect and encourage pupils' independent thinking can improve their self-esteem and may enhance motivation leading to a reduction of problems of control. With increased emphasis on problem solving and practical experiences, motivation may also be increased through negotiating tasks that have appeal to the individuals and that fall within the experiences of the pupils. The mathematics classroom can become a forum for the exchange of ideas with peer group discussion as well as teacher-pupil interactions. Opportunities to inquire and reflect will involve the pupils in decision making and in the construction of their own mathematical beliefs and strategies.

Within the new mathematics curriculum, practical skills in problem solving and presentation of findings must be valued alongside the more abstract notions that have typified much of the subject in the past. Take as an example pattern making and construction skills which may be used to initiate discussion of mathematical relationships with concrete and visual images to support hypotheses as well as mathematical formulae and calculations.

Richard, Adam and Colin found concentration difficult but enjoyed working with their practical tasks. Connecting cubes were used initially to discuss the geometric shape of a cube with experimentation to construct three different sized cubes. When a $2 \times 2 \times 2$ and $3 \times 3 \times 3$ cube had been made and further single cubes were in short supply, discussion arose about the number of individual cubes needed to make a $5 \times 5 \times 5$ cube. Even with a calculator, it was not possible for the trio to agree on a total and the teacher intervened to readdress the nature of each cube in stacked layers. With some difficulty, the $2 \times 2 \times 2$ and $3 \times 3 \times 3$ cubes were reconstructed as layers and represented on squared paper as a record of this task. It was at this point of representation that Colin analysed the pattern and used a calculator to add $25 + 25 + 25 + 25 + 25$. With 125 individual cubes, he set about his task of making a cube. Adam and Richard were initially frustrated by the shortage of cubes but a new supply was found to make colour patterned squares. These were recorded on squared paper and some interesting number patterns emerged. When the idea of enlarging squares was addressed, the following number pattern was discovered:

$1 + 3 = 4$
$1 + 3 + 5 = 9$
$1 + 3 + 5 + 7 = 16$

Although the square numbers and cube numbers did not appear to interest the boys at this stage, it is likely that some memory of these experiences will help to link numbers and shapes on some future occasion.

This task provided practical activity and discussion about cubes, their construction and volume. Patterns were identified and described both in the arrangements of colours and in the numerical relationships found. Algebra, geometry and number work were implicit for all and explicit for some of the trio who were challenged mathematically as well as being enthusiastic about the activity.

Within a problem solving environment, pupils may find themselves immersed in situations for which they do not possess all the necessary understanding. Then the pupils are encouraged to obtain information and master skills in order to solve a problem at hand, rather than because it happens to be the next topic in the curriculum. In these circumstances, pupils learn because of present relevance, 'here and now', rather than the 'it will be useful later' attitude so often found in mathematics teaching.

ORGANIZATION FOR LEARNING

The *Non-Statutory Guidance to the National Curriculum* (DES, 1989b) giving guidelines for the overall design and balance of a scheme of work includes the following:

5.2   Activities should bring together different areas of mathematics.
5.4   Activities should be a balance between tasks which develop knowledge, skills and understanding, and those which develop the ability to tackle practical problems.
5.10 Activities should be balanced between different modes of learning: doing, observing, talking and listening, discussing with other pupils, reflecting, drafting, reading and writing, etc.
5.14 Activities should enable, pupils to develop a positive attitude to mathematics. (B8–B11)

Suggestions are given for the way ' "closed" tasks to which there are specific answers to be obtained by specific methods' may be modified to 'produce more challenging "open" activities' (see Figure 2.1).

From the learner's perspective, an emphasis on independent thinking

CLOSED TASK	MODIFIED TASK
$2 + 6 - 3 =$	What numbers can you make from 2, 3 and 6?
$3 \times 5 =$	Make up some questions whose answer is 15.
Find the value of x	Investigate what the ⬛ sin button on a calculator does.
Continue this sequence: 1, 2, 4	Discuss how the sequence 1, 2, 4 . . . . . . might continue.
Find the area of this triangle.	Construct some triangles with the same area as this one.
What do we call a five-sided shape?	What shapes/configurations can you make with five lines?
Play a particular board-game.	Design a board game for four people, using a die and counters.
Draw the graphs of 1) $y = 3x + 5$ 2) $y = 2x - 4$ 3) $y = 6 - x$	Investigate the graphs of $y = ax + b$ for different values of a and b.
Copy and complete this addition table: 	Investigate the possible ways of completing this table:

Figure 2.1 *Comparison of closed and more open tasks*
Source: DES (1989b), D7.

and open-ended tasks may appear daunting to an individual whose confidence has been eroded by years of failure. Special needs pupils are often typified by poor organizational skills and lack of concentration, so the teacher must provide structures within which they can feel supported and valued for their contributions. Variations in teaching styles will be needed to develop a learning environment that encourages involvement and makes best use of each individual's contributions. Collaborative efforts at problem solving may elicit responses that involve discussion and negotiation. Games can provide non-threatening experiences that may be designed to involve substantial mathematics learning and recording may be undertaken as a group responsibility rather than an individual chore. Practical work and discussion are a requirement of the National Curriculum in mathematics and can help to develop social skills at the same time as giving the teacher opportunities for informal assessment, gaining further insight into the pupil's understanding.

SUMMARIZING THE CHANGES

One only needs to compare secondary school mathematics books (texts or pupil work) of the 1950s and 1960s with those of today to realise that 'drill and practice' through pages of sums have given way to exploration of patterns and relationships that exist in mathematics. From the time when mathematics was only available as an academic discipline for the privileged few to the 'mathematics for all' scene of today, changes in content and teaching styles have reflected the changing needs of society and better appreciation of the role that pupils may play in their own learning. The need for pupils to have a positive attitude to the subject and confidence to use mathematical skills in everyday problem solving has been highlighted in the Cockcroft Report which has been a cornerstone for establishing the principles for teaching mathematics today. Focus on pupils' ability to 'use and apply mathematics in practical tasks [and] in real-life problems' is explicit in the National Curriculum Draft Proposals (Dearing, 1994) which propose entitlement to a broad curriculum and an appropriate programme of study matched to the needs of each individual.

The principles for teaching mathematics outlined in this chapter relate to pupils who experience difficulty with learning just as much as any others, though the challenge for a teacher to incorporate many of the related objectives is intensified where special needs pupils are involved. Strategies to improve mathematics performance of low-attainers should involve the consistent and concerted efforts of teachers whose experiences with such pupils are supported by a sound knowledge and confidence in the subject of mathematics. In the Cockcroft Committee's guide for employers, *Blueprint for Numeracy* (DES, 1983) it is recommended that 'the most important resource for good mathematics teaching is an adequate supply of good mathematics teachers ... who have both ... mastery of mathematics ... and the capability to teach it'. This is reiterated in the more recent report *The Implementation of the Curricular Requirements of the Education Reform Act: Mathematics – Key Stages 1, 2, 3 and 4, the Fourth Year 1992–93* (OFSTED, 1993b) where Her Majesty's Chief Inspector reports that 'the quality of the teaching remains the single most important factor in the achievement of high standards and positive attitudes to work'. The combined efforts of a stable team of teachers with expertise in teaching pupils with special needs and mathematics specialists will generally be needed to meet the requirements of the National Curriculum in Mathematics today.

—3—

Psychology, pedagogy and mathematics

This chapter will explore some of the pedagogic developments that have taken place in mathematics education. In doing so it will trace elements of the psychological models which have come to influence teachers' action in classrooms. It is concerned with the influence of particular approaches to teaching on the perceived ability of pupils. The chapter will argue that the position of pupils with SEN in mainstream mathematics classrooms would be improved if they were taught in a way that is commensurate with contemporary models of pedagogy and curriculum content, rather than being 'treated' with restrictive pedagogies and narrow curricula. In doing so it will trace some of the history of the psychology of instruction in mathematics. This history is marked by a shift away from a consideration of the isolated passive individual responding to stimuli towards a consideration of the active social individual constructing meaning from, and in, a particular culture. The route is through the early twentieth-century behaviourism with its emphasis on drill and practice to the social constructivism of the latter part of the century. Along the way the chapter will touch on some aspects of the work of Gagné on learning hierarchies and Piaget and his influence on the so-called 'new maths' with limited reference to other influential models such as those based on theories of information processing. This is by no means an exhaustive consideration of this complex and convoluted field. Rather it is intended that this rapid tour should provide some signposts for further reading and raise some questions of direct relevance to the classroom practice of today. Above all the aim is to provide the reader with the psychological background to what became the 'common sense' of particular classroom practices.

At a time when common sense is used as a rationale for the promotion of particular styles of teaching it is perhaps as well to acknowledge that all common sense can be traced to a theoretical root and thus to a basis for making a critical response.

TRANSMISSION BASED PEDAGOGIES

Consideration of the many ways in which the teaching and learning processes have been theorized will help teachers to analyse the ways learning paradigms influence teaching approaches to mathematics and how changes in the curriculum may reflect psychological perspectives of learning.

Teaching is often equated with 'telling' and 'explaining' and it is assumed that children will gain knowledge when they 'have been told'. This approach has many shortcomings, not least the demonstrable evidence of failure in mathematics teaching over many generations where it has been implemented. In his general report for 1871 as a Schools Inspector, Matthew Arnold wrote:

> In every standard the rate of failure was greater than in 1869 . . . The rate of failure was highest in arithmetic still, as it always has been; the failure in this branch of study being five times as great as the failure in reading and twice as great as the failure in writing and spelling.
>   (Report on Elementary Schools, 1852–1882 (1910), p. 141)

Efforts to understand how children learn have informed more recent practice in the teaching of mathematics but any teacher knows that the problems have not been resolved and further reflection is important for future generations of school children. The Cockcroft Committee Report (DES, 1982) voices many complaints about low levels of mathematics, in particular numeracy, among young entrants to employment and quotes a Confederation of British Industry (CBI) spokesman:

> Mathematics . . . or arithmetic, which is really the primary concern . . . is the one area which is really brought up every time as a problem . . . This is the way in which shortfalls in the education of children makes itself most manifest immediately to an employer. (para. 43)

Drill and practice

For almost 100 years psychologists and educators have been investigating children's learning of arithmetic (which has accounted until recently for the majority of mathematics teaching). Behaviourists such as Thorndike analysed human behaviour in terms of stimulus and response. In applying this theory to arithmetic learning, Thorndike's book of 1913, *The Psychology of Arithmetic*, advocated establishing and strengthening associations through 'drill and practice'. The teacher's task was to identify the bonds required, to present them in appropriate sequence and to provide positive reinforcement and sufficient practice for the correct bonds to be learned. Thorndike's concern with the meaningfulness of a problem and its application to daily activities were that these were not integral but were seen as a reward in order to strengthen the bonds.

The pages of examples still to be found in many textbooks reflect this theory of learning but are usually now accompanied by concrete experiences and explanations of the underlying mathematical principles (see Figure 3.1). The strength of influence of these *transmission* based pedagogies is evident in the contemporary mathematics classroom. In their extreme version these practices assume that instruction may proceed in the absence of an understanding of the cognitive processing of that instruction by the pupil.

These early Behaviourist ideas were challenged by Brownell (1928) who advocated that learning should be achieved through meaningful instruction and understanding rather than drill and practice. 'If one is to be successful in quantitative thinking, one needs a fund of meanings not a myriad of automatic responses . . . drill does not develop meanings. Repetition does not lead to understanding' (Brownell, 1935). He stressed concepts and relationships so that children could apply better their knowledge, but he still focused on behaviour rather than proposing alternative ways in which knowledge may be acquired and teaching continued to be based on simple associations until the 1960s. Brownell also questioned the assumption that processes children use in arithmetic may be inferred from the processes adults use. This question will be familiar to all teachers who have engaged in trying to understand the methodologies special needs children bring to particular problems. A more recent contribution to the field of mathematics education which may be seen to have its roots in this work is that of Gagné (1965). His development of instructional hierarchies in mathematics have found a place in modern approaches to the curriculum which will be discussed below.

DEVELOPMENTAL MODELS

Contrasting this transmission model for learning is the view that knowledge is constructed by the learner who will try to rationalize experiences and incorporate acquired 'knowledge' into a personal framework of understanding. Historically, constructivism finds its roots embedded in the theories of many eminent psychologists whose theories of learning and development have influenced school teaching.

The case of Piaget

Undoubtedly the most fundamental influence this century on mathematics teaching has been that of Piaget whose theories of development provided the theoretical framework that has influenced mathematics

Calculate:

(a) 2.65×1.4

(b) $4.68 \div 0.6$

Solution:

(a)
$$
\begin{array}{r}
265 \\
\times \ \ 14 \\
\hline
1060 \\
2650 \\
\hline
3710
\end{array}
$$

Multiply, temporarily ignoring the decimal points.

There is a total of 3 decimal places in the question so there will be 3 decimal places in the answer. The answer is not complete until the correct number of decimal places has been shown.

Thus, $2.65 \times 1.4 = 3.710$ (3 decimal places in the answer).

(b) In $4.68 \div 0.6$ the divisor (0.6) is a decimal which makes the division awkward; it is asking 'How many times is 0.6 contained in 4.68?'
Thus we make the divisor a whole number by multiplying by 10, (i.e. $0.6 \times 10 = 6$).
We have multiplied 0.6 by 10 so we must also multiply 4.68 by 10, (i.e. $4.68 \times 10 = 46.8$).
Now the question reads $46.8 \div 6$.

$$
\begin{array}{r}
7.8 \\
6 \overline{)46.8}
\end{array}
$$
$$\therefore \ 4.68 \div 0.6 = 7.8$$

Exercise 1 K

Calculate the following:

1.	3.6×9	2.	4.7×8
3.	3.54×4	4.	83.2×6
5.	42×0.3	6.	72×0.2
7.	0.5×23	8.	0.5×2.3
9.	0.5×0.23	10.	5×0.023
11.	72.6×18	12.	39.5×13
13.	16.5×3.4	14.	23.9×6.8
15.	3.62×8.5	16.	4.49×7.3
17.	26.5×0.46	18.	43.2×0.71
19.	2.1×4.083	20.	6.7×1.709
21.	0.871×0.34	22.	0.927×0.18
23.	0.02×0.008	24.	0.05×0.0015
25.	$5.6 \div 8$	26.	$8.4 \div 7$
27.	$0.15 \div 5$	28.	$0.54 \div 6$
29.	$1.6 \div 0.4$	30.	$4.5 \div 0.9$
31.	$28 \div 0.7$	32.	$96 \div 0.4$
33.	$10 \div 0.8$	34.	$21 \div 0.8$
35.	$21.7 \div 0.4$	36.	$3 \div 0.08$

Figure 3.1 *'Drill and practice' type of exercise*
Source: Riddington and Grier (1981) *Blackwell Maths*, 2. Oxford: Blackwell, p. 9.

teaching and the mathematics curriculum from the 1960s.

Piaget (1952) maintained that children construct their own know-ledge through interactions with the environment developing a *cognitive structure* by way of organizing these experiences. This cognitive structure is not a static one but changes over time, developing through a series of 'stages' in a *predetermined* manner as a consequence of maturation and experience. Piaget's model is based on the notion that each individual engages in intellectual behaviour that indicates a specific way of reasoning. Each mode of reasoning being the outcome of the individual's 'cognitive structure', defining the limits of the child's intellectual functioning and determining the kind of logical thinking available to the child and hence the kinds of tasks which could be suc-cessfully handled (Piaget, 1952; Piaget and Inhelder, 1958). Cognitive development and transition from stage to stage occurs as the result of two processes: *assimilation*, whereby children incorporate new experiences into existing structures, and *accommodation* through which these existing structures are modified to incorporate new experiences. Learning takes place when the child is ready (adequately matured) to assimilate a number of experiences which lead to a 'spon-taneous cognitive reorganisation'. Piaget thus made a distinction between physical knowledge and logico-mathematical knowledge. Through the processes of empirical abstraction (abstraction of proper-ties from objects) and reflective abstraction (involving the construc-tion of relationships between and among objects) logico-mathematical frameworks develop. These frameworks bring new knowledge into relation with existing knowledge (assimilation) and may themselves be transformed (accommodation).

Despite the considerable amount of attention that is given to Piaget's work in the field of mathematics education he made very little reference to teaching method. His was an exploration of the processes involved in mathematical learning. The Piagetian adventure may be seen as a psychological consequence of an early twentieth-century debate in the philosophy of mathematics. Piaget presents education with *a* theory of logico-mathematical development rather than *the* theory as it has tended to be regarded.

His influence on the classroom certainly marked a departure from the transmission model in which students are thought to modify their internal models of mathematical matters in such a way as to mirror those which are held by their teachers. This transmission model of communication in the classroom gave way to a Piagetian version of a constructivist approach where the teachers role changed from 'trans-ferring' knowledge to building with the child a conceptual framework for understanding. The educational implication of this theoretical position is that as children develop their own understanding through empirical and reflective abstraction, mathematical concepts cannot be directly taught. Rather it is the teacher's role to build an educational environment which will stimulate the processes of logico-mathematical development. Associated with this position is the understanding that the state of logico-mathematical development conditions the possibilities for learning. Children have to be conceptually *ready* to learn. There is no point in trying to teach something to a child who is not ready to learn it. This view can lead to lack of pupil progress being viewed as a problem located within the child rather than in the form of instruction. A Piagetian rationale may be resorted to when a child fails to make progress. If this happens explorations of curriculum and pedagogic change may be abandoned in favour of allowing the child more time to develop. Perhaps not the best strategy for a child who almost by definition needs to maximize its rate of learning.

There have been several contributions to the literature which provide alternatives to the practice of waiting for a learner to be ready to develop. Case and Bereiter (1984) summarize attempts to take account of the strengths of the task analysis approach and incorporate into it developmental considerations. They lay emphasis on the need for the teacher to work from an understanding of the way in which learners approach problems unaided which may contrast with expectations derived from models of learning. They also caution that working memory requirements of specific learning hierarchies should be considered when teaching and learning programmes are being designed.

Bruner and Dienes

Other psychologists have sought to provide a developmental account which benefited from the Piagetian opus and yet announced a more positive role for instruction. Bruner (1967) brought together knowledge of experimental psychology with classroom practice to propose a theory based on three modes of cognitive (mental) representation in which children progress from *enactive* representation, actively manipulating concrete materials, to *iconic* to pictorial representation involving mental images and ultimately *symbolic* represention with competent use of language and mathematical symbols. Bruner (1960) did not advocate the notion of 'readiness' before moving on but rather suggested that anything can be presented in a simple enough form for a child to understand in a spiral curriculum model of learning. Enactive and iconic modes are not superseded by symbolic modes, rather they assume new and developing roles as the spiral unfurls. Bruner's work is also positioned within the general 'catch all' of constructivism. That is he assumes that knowledge is actively constructed by the learner in the form of connected mental representations. His work is informed by a concern for the underlying principles and logical organisation of mathematics. Experiences with concrete materials and pictorial representation are widely used to support computational practice in mathematics learning in what became known as the structuralist approach:

> The curriculum of a subject should be determined by the most fundamental understanding that can be achieved of the underlying principles that give structure to the subject. Teaching specific *procedures* or skills without making clear their context in the broader fundamental structure of a field is uneconomical in several deep senses. In the first place, such teaching makes it exceedingly difficult for the student to generalise from what he has learned to what he will encounter later. In the second place, learning that has fallen short of a group of general principles has little reward in terms of intellectual excitement . . . Third, knowledge one has acquired without sufficient structure to tie it together is knowledge that is likely to be forgotten.
>
> (from Bruner, 1960)

Dienes (1960), who worked closely with Bruner, stresses the concrete to abstract progression in learning and concerns himself with the child's motivation and perception of activities as enjoyable and intrinsically worthwhile. A lasting contribution to classroom mathematics has been the arithmetic blocks he designed to provide apparatus for arithmetic and which may be found in many classrooms and illustrations in mathematics texts today. Dienes argued that structural aspects of mathematics are acquired as they engage in activities with materials that embody the concepts which are the object of instruction. However, as Holt (1982) points out, the assumption that learners will invariably construct appropriate understandings on the basis of experience with manipulative materials may not be well founded. He questions how learners are supposed to apprehend the mathematical relationships embodied in instructional materials if they are not already aware of them:

> Children who already understood base and place value, even if only intuitively, could see the connections between written numerals and these blocks . . . But children who could not do these problems without the blocks didn't have a clue about how to do them with the blocks . . . They found the blocks . . . as abstract, as disconnected from reality, mysterious, arbitrary, and capricious as the numbers that these blocks were supposed to bring to life. (p. 28)

Arguably one of the main effects of the structuralist approach in school mathematics has been an emphasis on conceptual and notational formalism that proves to debar all but the most able from the principled understanding that is intended. The schemes that were produced to structuralist specifications such as *Modern Mathematics for Schools* and to a lesser extent the *Kent Mathematics Project* were seen to be very demanding on teachers. As Macnab and Cummine (1986) point out 'it requires teachers who are themselves actively interested in the subject, who both understand the broad general principles of mathematics and appreciate their importance and who are willing to plan their teaching around these principles' (p. 4). It remains open to question the extent to which teachers working in secondary schools with pupils whose attainments are low in mathematics feel confident that a structural approach is appropriate for them as teachers and ultimately for the pupils they teach. Sadly an initiative which attempted to help pupils acquire the principles of mathematics was often seen to result in a practice which was rather formalistic and in which children experienced an unconnected series of exercises from which they found it hard to abstract meaning. Although abstraction in not automatic and pupils may experience difficulties generalizing, verbalizing and ultimately symbolizing the relationships embodied in such apparatus, practical tasks with 'concrete materials' provide one of the experiences pupils may draw on to develop understanding in mathematics. Generally, activities providing tactile experiences and visual images may form the basis of discussions and promote pupil participation in their own learning. Relating classroom tasks to real world problems will rely on discussions involving explicit connections where the role of the teacher is to encourage generalizations and applications of developing skills. In classrooms today, the connections between arithmetic procedures involving 'concrete materials' and the results of parallel procedures on a calculator may provide the basis for investigations. (Where the materials are real coins, calculators can not only provide fast and accurate answers to problems but may also help pupils understand the decimal representation and its currency counterpart.)

Skemp

Understanding in mathematics is something which evolves and develops with experience. There is no clear point where understanding suddenly happens and it is true that understanding in mathematics is probably never complete. Understanding advances when new ideas and insights are related to existing experiences. Skemp (1971), a mathematician who wrote *The Psychology of Learning Mathematics*, stressed the importance of relating new ideas to what has already been grasped in a somewhat different view of structuralism in mathematics. He distinguishes between *relational* and *instrumental* understanding: in the former, new ideas are integrated into existing schemata so that the child knows 'what to do and why', whereas instrumental understanding enables the child to get correct answers but can be summed up as 'rules without reasons'. Both are classed as forms of understanding but rote-memorized rules and the manipulation of symbols with little or no meaning are not only boring but are harder to learn than an integrated meaningful structure. Able pupils benefit by being able to construct their own meanings and connections, those with lower ability need substantial support if meaningful learning is to take place. Skemp also distinguished types of learning as 'intelligent' learning and 'rote' learning (rote memorization) although he acknowledged that the two may be difficult to distinguish. He proposes 'schematic learning' in preference to 'just memorizing the manipulation of symbols' and identifies the role of the teacher as helping to 'lay a well-structured foundation of basic mathematical ideas, on which the learner can build in whatever future direction becomes necessary'.

These theories together point to the necessity of identifying the understanding and skills already possessed by the child in order to build on an existing framework of knowledge and the type of learning that may be taking place. Children are not 'empty vessels' but thinking individuals whose interest must be stimulated and whose thinking must be channelled. It is clear that instruction does affect what children learn but it does not determine it. When successful, children actively structure, interpret and assimilate incoming information as they attempt to fit it into their existing framework of knowledge.

Vygotsky and Social-Constructivism

Many researchers have acknowledged that relationships and inter-pretations are constructed within an environment of shared inter-pretation, negotiation and communication. Children's mathematics learning will be mediated by interactions with parents and family as well as peers and teachers and the child will construct meaning via social negotiation, meaning being communicated as a social product. This brings to the forefront a need to consider social groupings, language and representation as vital factors affecting mathematics learning.

Vygotsky (1981) emphasised the roles of social interaction and ver-bal communication in the learning of mathematics. A central tenet of Vygotsky's theory is the idea that all psychological structures are created through interaction with the social environment. Vygotsky's General Genetic Law of Cultural Development stresses the notion that in order to understand higher mental processes an investigator must examine their social origins:

> Any function in the child's cultural development appears twice, or on two planes. First it appears on the social plane, and then on the psychological plane.
>
> (from Vygotsky, 1978)

Vygotsky argued that higher mental functions must be viewed as the products of mediated activity. Psychological tools and the means of interpersonal communication served as mediators of social forces and factors within his theoretical framework. Psychological tools such as language or number systems are used in the course of cognitive development. This linkage between mathematical cognition and cultural practices is now widely recognized. Cultural differences in mathematical activities such as counting have been studied (e.g. Saxe *et al.*, 1984; Saxe *et al.*, 1988) and the transfer of learning across cultural practices has been considered (Saxe, 1989). These findings are analogous with the studies that have compared mathematical strategies which have their origins 'on the street' with those required in school (Carraher *et al.*, 1985).

Studies of large scale social components of what is learned have been complimented by smaller scale studies which have promoted an understanding of interactional, rather than a societal, social component of learning (Kent, 1978; Lampert, 1986; Greeno, 1986; Ginsburg and Yamamoto, 1986). Walden and Walkerdine (1985) made a major contribution to the understanding of the process of gender differentiation in mathematics classes. It has been shown that the criteria of competence required and recognized in mathematics classrooms acted as a source of discrimination, bias and disadvantage. There have been several attempts to resolve home/school cultural differences in approaches to mathematics. These have done much to promote the acceptance of the need to understand and respond to such differences (Jones and Haylock, 1985; Hughes, 1986). Within special education the implications of the cultural conflicts underpinning communication difficulty have been shown to have implications for the teaching and learning of mathematics (Daniels, 1990; Erting, 1985).

The implications for mathematical education are considerable. Vygotsky's well-known concept of the Zone of Proximal Development, within which the child is receptive of new relationships to supplement and support existing ones, stresses the need for educational settings which involve co-operation *and* guidance:

> The distance between the actual developmental level as determined by independent problem solving and the level of potential development as determined through problem solving under adult guidance or in collaboration with more capable peers.
>
> (from Vygotsky, 1978)

What emerges from this definition is the notion of guided interaction which is responsive to individual learning needs. When communication becomes the focus of attention, the role of linguistic communication becomes a way of guiding the child's learning, not transferring knowledge (Kilpatrick, 1987). Children's deviations from teachers' expectations become a means for understanding their efforts to make sense of mathematical relationships and miscommunication can inform as much as successful communication in promoting learning.

Learning need must bear some relation to the amount and type of informal knowledge that the child brings into school. This position acknowledges that mathematical activity is a social as well as a cognitive phenomenon and that everyday mathematical practices can differ from one social/cultural group to another. However, it seems that schools have difficulty in responding to social and cultural diversity at the level of informal mathematical knowledge:

> It seems that children treat arithmetic class as a setting in which to learn rules, but are somehow discouraged from bringing to school their informally acquired knowledge about number . . . The process of schooling seems to encourage the idea that . . . there is not supposed to be much continuity between what one knows outside school and what one learns in school.
>
> (Resnick, 1987, p. 15)

It is clear that some children develop strategic approaches to solving mathematical problems which are *not* compatible with school-based procedures. Evidence of this kind of behaviour is given in a variety of recent studies, notably Ginsburg and Allardice (1984) and Carraher *et al.* (1985). It seems that children come to understand aspects of the application of mathematical knowledge in different ways depending on their interpretation of the demands of their immediate situation. This approach to the analysis of the relationship between everyday and school-based knowledge has been at one time cast in terms of deficiency and at others in terms of difference. There are those, Baroody (1984), who argue that children who have deficiencies in informal knowledge are likely to have learning difficulties in school.

Vygotsky argues that all psychological processes are initially social. This socialization/regulation by others, before a child is able to gain conscious use of a particular bit of knowledge, is referred to as 'other-regulation'. Other-regulation occurs on the inter psychological plane, prior to internalization of the knowledge by the learner. In addition, other-regulation occurs in the first stage of Vygotsky's theory of verbal self-regulation. Self-regulation occurs in the second and third stages of Vygotsky's theory of verbal self-regulation. Teaching and learning again becomes a matter of transfer. This time the transfer is that of control from the teacher to the learner.

Vygotsky's three stages of verbal self-regulation are:

1. External – when children are regulated by the verbalization of a more experienced member of society.
2. Egocentric (private speech) – when children talk aloud to themselves to bring behaviour under verbal control. First children act, then talk about the activity, next they act and speak to themselves

simultaneously, finally they use self-verbalization in a purposeful, deliberate way to regulate their subsequent behaviour.
3. Internal (inner speech)-language to self is covert, silent, inhibited speech-to-self.

At each of these stages the pupils with SEN are perhaps at more risk than many in their peer group. Years of failure and frustration despite efforts to learn results in lack of respect for 'authority in mathematical truth' or an inability to identify with the social interactions that lead to reflection and learning. Positive efforts need to be made to nurture and value any exposition of personal thinking.

The use of words to intervene between stimulus and response for the learner is crucial because they act as mediators. Speech is reversible because words can be both stimulus (heard word) and response. Thus the process of internalization is *not* simple copying. It involves the active interpretation and transformation of instruction.

Leont'ev (1981) develops the idea that pupils have their own ways of working on learning. He emphasizes the fact that they should also benefit from instruction which focuses on the learning activity. Without the influence of a structured approach to instruction the pupil will find it a struggle to learn in a way that is not hampered by the constraints of the immediate social circumstances. This is not to argue a case for instructional imposition or even to suggest the existence of an ideal instructional package or sequence. Within the Vygotskian model, the appropriation process is always a two-way process. The content of instruction will be mediated and then internalized *not* copied. Cobb *et al.* (1992) present an approach to this kind of pedagogy that avoids the traps of both consensual *laissez-faire* and over-determined instructional procedures.

In this characterization of the learning/teaching process, teachers as well as students modify their interpretations in the light of their developing understandings of each others' mathematical activity. This is not to deny that the teachers are necessarily an authority in the classroom in that only they can assess the potential fruitfulness of students' individual and collective activity for their future learning 'it is by capitalizing on students' mathematical activity that the teacher initiates and guides the classroom community's development of taken-as-shared ways of mathematical knowing that are compatible with those of the wider community' (Cobb *et al.*, 1992, p. 11).

Saxe (1991) develops an approach which incorporates key elements of Piagetian constructivism (assimilation and accommodation in self-regulated goal setting) into the neo-Vygotskian socio-cultural account. His interest lies in the consideration of constructive mechanisms by which goals and understandings develop as part of socio-cultural activity. This important thesis provides a good example of the way in which psychological traditions may come to enrich each other. There is a certain convenience in writing a review such as this to ignore the interaction between traditions. However, it is clearly the case that many of the approaches discussed in this chapter have had considerable impact on each other. As Bidell (1992) argues 'the crucial issue on which Piaget's stage theory and Vygotsky's sociohistorical theory differ is not simply whether the social dimension of development is considered, rather, it is the question of how *relations* between the social and the personal is conceptualised' (p. 306). Bidell distinguishes between Piaget's *stage theory* of development and his *constructivist theory* of knowledge. He proceeds to argue that 'the subject-object unity and participatory character of Piaget's constructivism implicitly supports a contextualist approach to knowledge development and stands in contradiction to the individualism and interactionism of his stage theory' (p. 307).

Saxe develops a view of cognitive development as a process which is driven by that which is socially and culturally available in line with the neo-Vygotskian tradition but which retains elements of the Piagetian version of constructivism. His approach is comprised of three components as shown below:

1. the dynamic processes of goal formation in everyday cultural practices;
2. cognitive developments linked to children's goal directed activities;
3. a concern with the interplay between children's learning across contexts and practices.

(from Saxe et al., 1993)

Throughout Saxe *et al.* emphasize the need to focus on the relation between the constructive activities of the child and the social and cultural processes in which they are embedded.

INFORMATION PROCESSING

In the 1970s considerable research was undertaken concerning mathematical thinking. A shift in theories of learning could be observed, away from behaviourism and rote learning through drill and practice towards cognitivism and a more conceptual approach (Resnick and Ford, 1981; Schoenfeld, 1988), emphasizing the learner's active involvement in the step-by-step processing of information (Wittrock, 1974). Issues of automaticity, where responses are available instantly, have been raised in many of the information processing models of cognitive processes. These models share a concern for the way in which the architecture of the mind operates on data. Information processing approaches introduce concepts of planning, executive control and selective attention into a field which had previously considered only responses to stimuli. Using the metaphor of the electronic computer they develop the notion of the human as an information processing system which is limited by constraints of various memory stores and processor speeds etc. The limits of the information processing system (human mind) impose what are referred to as channel capacities. Humans are thought to develop strategies for working around and within these limits. For example, information may be chunked into smaller packages in order that working memory restrictions may be eased. The faster that information is organized into chunks, or encoded, the more likely it is that complex problems will be solved. The larger the chunks the more information working memory can handle. Thus the organization of knowledge to allow for such chunking becomes a priority with a strictly limited working memory. The less attention that has to be devoted to an item the more processing capacity is left available for the rest of a task. Frank Smith (1971) has become well known for his application of such models to the reading process. Children who experience difficulty with learning in mathematics tend to use time, and working memory, using counting strategies for solving basic arithmetic problems rather than retrieving remembered number bond facts. Additionally they are more likely to establish incorrect number facts in memory:

> Thus children who initially make many errors may subsequently make more retrieval errors because the incorrect associations will be established between a problem and its result.
>
> (Dockrell and McShane, 1993, p. 132)

Thus the question of the role of drill and practice in a balanced pedagogic menu is not simply dealt with by references to a time when it was felt to fulfil all needs. If some version of an information processing model is accepted then it follows that if some basic processes can be carried out automatically then the limits of working memory may not be exceeded in higher order problem solving. The focus of teaching concern may be with speed and depth of processing and it may be that drill and practice may come to find a place within a broader framework of influences.

There is good reason to believe that automaticity with respect to, say, number bonds provides significant advantages in advanced arithmetic calculation. From an experimental and an intuitive point of view this would seem to be sensible (Resnick and Ford, 1981). However, the question must be addressed as to whether drill and practice is the appropriate means for establishing such automatic facility.

Drill and practice may be distinguished from reinforcement tasks if distinction is made between rote and meaningful learning that is involved. There are certainly many arguments against rote learning which is not meaningful for the pupils. As well as adversely affecting attitudes and motivation, it is questionable how valuable rote learning may be. Ausubel presents a powerful argument in favour of meaningful learning:

> The crucial difference between rote and meaningful learning categories has important implications for the kind of learning and retention process underlying each category. Since rote-learned materials do not interact with the cognitive structure in a substantive, organic fashion . . . their retention is influenced primarily by the interfering effects of *similar* rote materials learned *immediately* before and after the learning task. Learning and retention outcomes in the case of meaningful learning, on the other hand, are influenced primarily by the properties of those relevant and cumulatively established ideational systems in cognitive structure with which the learning task interacts and which determine its dissociability strength.
>
> (from Ausubel, 1968)

He identifies arguments to suggest the superiority of meaningful learning, in that learning and retention are easier and transferability to other tasks, is enhanced. Where rote learning has taken place, pupils are able to apply this to a limited set of tasks closely related to the learned task. Memory is limited by identifying discrete, unconnected skills where connections have not been made and recall may lead to confusion in selecting and applying appropriate procedures. Ausubel also notes that in meaningful learning the materials are not *already* meaningful but only *potentially* meaningful. The very object of meaningful learning is to convert potential meaning into actual (psychological) meaning. Within this constraint, the role of the teacher is to present meaningful tasks and engage with pupils to ensure meaningful learning is taking place.

LEARNING HIERARCHIES

The complexity of mathematics learning was acknowledged by Gagné (1965) who attempted to identify elements of simple tasks which function as elements of more complex tasks and proposed learning hierarchies of ordered skills with prerequisite sub skills. Gagné identified eight kinds of learning which can be applied to mathematical tasks, each being a prerequisite for the next: signal learning, stimulus-response learning, chaining, verbal associations, multiple discrimination, concept learning (making a common response to a class of stimuli in terms of some common abstract property), principle learning (forming a chain of two or more concepts) and problem solving. The implications for instruction are that tasks should be broken down into components which should be presented in sequence to develop understanding in progressive stages. In doing this, instruction is developed on the basis of a notion of transfer in which relatively simple learning forms the basis for, and assists, more complex learning. Irrespective of the complexity of the task it is argued that mastery may be achieved by providing the learner with a hierarchy of subtasks developed through a task analysis undertaken by the teacher or course designer. The development need not be step-by-step and alternative routes may be appropriate, but understanding builds towards the goal of complex problem solving. Learning hierarchies carry with them strong implications for teaching and assessment. Their very nature is suggestive of an order for instruction. Curriculum-based assessment referenced to learning hierarchies can provide information for the skilled teacher about the way in which individual learners skip elements and take alternative routes. Hierarchies can be used as the basis for decision making concerning individual needs for instruction.

Klahr and Wallace (1973) and Schaeffer *et al.* (1974) suggest a *skill integrationist* model in which cognitive skills are built on earlier skills, new knowledge being acquired when integration of learned skills permits increasing generalization to new situations. This would suggest that practice and co-ordination of skills, for example in problem solving, that are generalization-directed rather than goal-directed, will lead to increased integration and to acquisition of higher level concepts and skills. This work is often associated with the possibility of conducting rational task analyses for the purpose of constructing hierarchies based on what is intuited or logically deduced about human information processing and task performance (see Resnick and Ford (1981)). Such task analyses, based on what psychology suggests happens in mathematical learning, contrasts with empirical task analysis which is based on observations of what children actually do, or appear to do. Rational task analysis may provide teachers with a logical basis for the analysis of children's difficulties.

When researching the understanding of number concepts in low attaining seven to nine-year-olds, Denvir (1986) attempted to identify a framework which describes pupils' order of acquisition of number concepts and devise teaching and activities which would extend pupils' understanding of number. Using a categorization of word problems given by Riley *et al.* (1983), a hierarchical framework of inter-related skills was constructed and diagnostic tests used to establish what understanding of number individual pupils already possessed (see Figures 3.2 and 3.3).

A teaching programme was implemented to 'teach' skills which were considered to be 'next skills' in the hierarchy or further on in the hierarchy and the pupils acquisition of skills were later tested. The results showed that such an approach was useful for describing each pupil's knowledge of number and in establishing which cognitive skills were most likely to be learned. However, it was less useful as a predictor

3. Mentally carries out two-digit 'take away' with regrouping
6. Uses multiplication facts to solve a 'sharing' word problem
47. Perceives 'compare (more) difference unknown' word problem as subtraction
4. Models two-digit 'take away' with regrouping using 'base ten' apparatus
45. Appreciates concept of class inclusion, without any hint or help
7. Mentally carries out two-digit take away without regrouping
5. Uses multiplication facts to solve a 'lots of' word problem
2. Mentally carries out two-digit addition with regrouping
20. Uses counting back/up/down strategy for 'take away'
33. Bundles objects to make a new group of ten in order to facilitate enumeration of a collection which is partly grouped in 10s and 1s
15. Uses repeated addition or repeated subtraction for a 'sharing' word problem
46. Partly appreciates concept of class inclusion
12. Uses derived facts for addition
8. Mentally carries out two-digit addition without regrouping
24. Can repeat the number sequence for counting in 10s from a non-decade two-digit number
25. Can repeat the number sequence for counting backwards in 10s from a non-decade two-digit number
34. Makes quantitative comparison between two collections which are grouped differently
9. 'Knows answer' when taking ten away from a two-digit number
10. 'Knows answer' when adding ten to a two-digit number
1. Models two-digit addition with regrouping using 'base ten' apparatus
17. Knows number bonds (not just the 'doubles')
26. Interpolates between decade numbers on a number line
13. Models two-digit 'take away' without regrouping using 'base ten' apparatus
16. Uses repeated addition for a 'lots of' word problem
19. Solves 'compare (more) difference unknown' word problem
21. Counts in 2s and 1s to enumerate a collection grouped in 2s and 1s
11. 'Knows answer' when adding units to a decade number
14. Models two-digit addition without regrouping using 'base ten' apparatus
22. Counts in 5s and 1s to enumerate a collection grouped in 5s and 1s
18. Solves 'compare (more) compared set unknown' word problem
23. Counts in 10s and 1s to enumerate a collection grouped in 10s and 1s
40. Knows numbers backwards from 20
27. Orders a selection of non-sequential two-digit numerals
35. Appreciates structure of grouped collections
38. Solves sharing problems by direct physical modelling
39. Solves 'lots of' problems by direct physical modelling
44. Appreciates conservation of number
28. Appreciates commutativity of addition for sums of the form $1 + n$
29. Uses a counting-on strategy for addition
30. Reads a selection of non-sequential two-digit numerals
32. Repeats numbers in correct sequence for counting in 2s, 5s and 10s
37. Uses counting-on strategy when provoked
31. Repeats numbers in correct sequence to 99
41. Knows numbers backwards from ten
36. Compares collections and states whether equal
42. Can say numbers in correct sequence to 20, can solve addition and take away by direct physical modelling
43. Makes 1 : 1 correspondence

Figure 3.2 *Hierarchy of some skills in arithmetic, assessed in order of difficulty (hardest first)*
Source: Denvir (1986), p. 30.

of precisely which, or how many, skills a pupil actually learned. Some of the individuals involved did not acquire the skills being taught but made progress in different parts of the hierarchical framework.

Although teachers can be sure of those skills they are attempting to teach, it became clear that it was not at all certain which skills would actually be learned. Even with a detailed hierarchy, predicting what pupils will learn is not certain, *teaching will affect what is learned but cannot determine it.*

USING HIERARCHIES TO DESIGN PROGRAMMES OF STUDY

The process of task analysis is central to the construction of many of the syllabuses and programmes of work to be found in schools today. It has also been central in the development of individual programmes for children with SEN. Ainscow and Tweddle (1979) provide an example of the application of this approach to special needs education in general. There have been many critiques of this approach, not least by Ainscow and Tweddle (1988), which focus on the potential within this approach for excessive attention to the individual at the expense of a wider systems/whole school view. However, there are also questions about the validity of simplistic task analytic methods for mathematics in particular.

The assumption that a learner assembles individual task components into a complete package in itself presents some potential difficulties with respect to the learning of mathematics. These are made manifest if and when a particular learner gets 'stuck' at a particular stage in a learning hierarchy. The motivation for pursuing a particular sub goal of the overall task is to be found in the logic of the analysis itself In some cases it may not be at all clear to a learner why they are attempting to solve a particular stage in an analysis, the ultimate purpose of which is obscure. Put simply, a child may not know *why on earth* it is being required to perform a particular task.

In its crudest form the task analytic approach is silent on the method of achieving success. Methods may be employed at certain stages only to be abandoned at others. The more complex the overall mathematical goal the more likely the need for a shift in method. If learners become too tightly bound to prior methods they may not be able to make subsequent progress.

As is so often the case it has been in the process of implementation that much of Gagné's work has become problematic. If task analysis is used in the classroom as a process for clarifying and understanding the pupil's learning then it can become an invaluable support for a reflective teacher. The process involves making teaching intuitions explicit, in the form of proposed learning sequences. These proposed

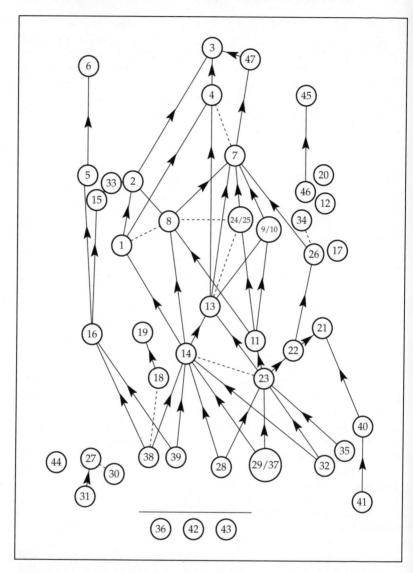

Figure 3.3 *Descriptive framework:* (n) *indicates skill* n *in Figure 3.2,* (m)——▶(n) *indicates skill* m *is pre-requisite for skill* n, *and* (i) – – –(j) *indicates strong connection between skill* i *and skill* j. *Source:* Denvir (1986), p. 33.

instructional sequences then form the basis of a teaching/learning experiment in which pupil responses are used as data which are fed back into the instructional design phase. Teaching becomes problem solving. Teaching sequences are regarded as the object of teacher/ researcher activity.

Sadly, there have been too many instances of examples of teaching objectives (for example those offered in Ainscow and Tweddle (1979)) being literally photocopied and used inflexibly as definitive instructional pathways. All the power of the approach as a heuristic device is lost. Task analyses become 'cast in tablets of stone' and the possibility of modification for individual learners is lost. In this way the learning hierarchy can come to take the dialogue out of teaching. Whatever the pupils do they are faced with the same set of instructions. It is not clear as to why mathematics classrooms can become rigid and inflexible in this way. Various writers have offered suggestions such as insecurity about the subject matter; pressure of time; and inappropriate understanding of the nature of learning difficulty (Larcombe, 1985; Macnab and Cummine, 1986; Resnick and Ford, 1981). Suffice it to say that the strengths of the learning hierarchy approach will be realized in a classroom situation in which the teacher is looking for tools with which to understand the learning process rather than programmes to follow.

'DISABLED' BY THE CURRICULUM?

Baroody and Hume (1991) argue that most children who experience difficulty learning mathematics are victims of instruction that is not suited to how children think and learn. They invoke the notion of children becoming 'curriculum disabled'. The interactional or transactional model of SEN discussed in Chapter 1 argues for an understanding of the causes of learning difficulty which takes account of within child **and** environmental factors in a dynamic system of interchanges. The notion of curriculum disability may be taken to be a simple environmental account. This is perhaps not a helpful reading of the concept. It would perhaps be better to consider the work of Baroody and Hume as one which establishes *the case for* an interactive model given that so many of the practices in mathematics education have either explicitly or implicitly announced a conventional within person deficit model of causation. All children can become 'curriculum disabled' in one setting or another, the important matter for teachers is not to lose sight of the fact that failure should not be thought of simply in terms of pathology or circumstance. This echoes the concept of 'curriculum mismatch' explored by Bennett (1987) in his work on the quality and level of task set in classrooms. 'There is little to be gained from high pupil involvement on tasks that are either not comprehensible or worthwhile'.

Put simply these writers suggest that if mathematics education was improved in general then the position of a considerable proportion of children who experience noticeable difficulty in learning would be significantly enhanced. Importantly, Baroody and Hume also allow for the possibility that a much smaller number of pupils may require special instructional methods.

TEACHING IMPLICATIONS

It is possible to understand how mathematics as we know it came into being (Resnick and Ford, 1981). It is also possible to provide general descriptions about groupings of mathematical attainments as they occur in development (Piaget, 1953). It is not possible to provide teachers with clear, unambiguous information about how individuals learn and come to understand mathematics. This may always be the case if theories concerning the mediation of social effects in learning prove to be valid. The evidence of the existence of variation in strategic approaches to learning may be taken as evidence in support of such social constructionism. The theoretical antecedents of much of the practice of the teaching of mathematics may still be traced to an individualist perspective. If, following Vygotsky, individual learning is to be construed as the internalized results of social activity mediated through sign systems such as speech then we need to place instructional methods in a social position. This position must be one in which instructional dialogues are seen as the means by which learners may be introduced to the mathematical culture of their teachers. Teachers can also come to understand and respond to the range of social understandings that will be brought to them by their pupils.

Thus the development of mathematical understanding for special needs pupils requires a co-ordinated programme of activities within a social context in which meanings can be negotiated and individuals are respected for their contributions even when these are not central to a preplanned outcome. Planning must integrate all contributions from teachers and support teams. The role of the human mediators, within school and outside, between an individual and their experiences must be seen to be as crucial as the representation and language used to communicate the mathematical ideas. The classroom can become a forum for shared activity with negotiated outcomes and diversity in the communication of ideas. Crucially it also requires clarity about what counts as mathematical knowing in the wider community.

Learning may be thought of as a process by which students modify their internal models of mathematical matters in such a way as to mirror those which are held by their teachers. This *transmission* model of communication is in contrast to the ever growing range of *constructivist* approaches within which pupils construct and modify their own knowledge in the light of experiences. This range of constructivist models moves from those such as Piaget's which posits a pregiven logico-mathematical invariant, to those such as Laves (1988) which dispenses with developmental imperatives and cedes influence to the specific discourse in which the learner is positioned. Arguably the twentieth century has witnessed the theoretical enhancement of the child as an active learner as part of a culturally situated community rather than an isolated individual, as a constructor of knowledge rather than a receiver. The teachers' role within this theoretical shift has been transformed from the transmitter of pregiven understanding to the mediator between informal meanings and those which are taken to be socially valued at a particular time. At all times it is appropriate to be aware that what is 'real' for children is the reality of their own experiences.

It has been pointed out (Pirie and Kieren, 1992) that although constructivism is not a set of rules to follow or actions to perform, there are shared beliefs that will help foster a creative classroom environment for mathematics learning. They identify four beliefs:

1. Although a teacher may have the intention to move a student towards particular mathematics learning goals, she will be well aware that such progress may not be achieved as expected by others.
2. In creating an environment or providing opportunities for children to modify their mathematical understanding, the teacher will act upon the belief that there are different pathways to similar mathematical understanding.
3. The teacher will be aware that different people will hold different mathematical understandings.
4. The teacher will know that for any topic there are different levels of understanding, but that these are never achieved 'once and for all'. (pp. 507–8)

Understanding of a topic is not an acquisition, it is an ongoing process which is by nature unique to each individual student. Where a teacher holds a 'constructivist' perspective on learning, different understandings and different levels of understanding lead a teacher to look beyond correct responses to routine questions and to seek and even enjoy the surprise of different understandings in individual students.

4

Classroom applications

In this chapter we will focus primarily on teaching approaches that enable a broadening of the curriculum for those pupils with learning difficulties in mathematics who are frequently referred to as 'low attainers'. We will consider the need for appropriate practical work as well as problem solving approaches to develop mathematical thinking and provide the basis for communication. The role of group work will be addressed alongside various approaches to social interaction that may enhance pupils' learning. In this chapter we will also present arguments for the use of games as a valuable aid to learning in the mathematics classroom.

WHAT MATHEMATICS IS BEING TAUGHT?

Early reports on the implementation of the National Curriculum indicated that there had been some shift towards broadening the curriculum for low-attainers. In the main findings of the report of HMI on the first year, 1989–90 of implementation of Key Stage 1 and 3 Mathematics (HMI, 1991) it was stated that 'a broader curriculum was being planned, particularly for pupils in Key Stage 1 and low-achieving pupils in Key Stage 3'. The report went on to acknowledge also that 'A major challenge was to provide a mathematics curriculum for low-achieving pupils which was sound and balanced across all the ATs and not restricted to number and measures'.

However, Her Majesty's Chief Inspector (OFSTED, 1993b) reports more recently that 'time spent on number in some of the schools was excessive and ineffective'. As it is being implemented currently, the National Curriculum for low-attainers in mathematics still appears to act as a constraint within which pupils may experience a very limited curriculum, based largely on repetition of skills they failed to master in primary school.

Yet in criteria for the content of mathematics, *Mathematics From 5 to 16* (HMI, 1985) recommend:

it is most important that pupils of low attainment are not restricted to a purely arithmetical diet . . . there must be sufficient breadth to enable a network of content to be established in the pupils' minds. Mathematics for all pupils, including low attainers, should certainly include a considerable geometrical component with work in both two and three dimensions . . . Algebraic ideas can also emerge where the need to make concise statements arises naturally. (p. 29)

This statement precedes, and is reflected in, legislation within the Education Reform Act (1988) and the subsequent Statutory Orders requiring study of five aspects of mathematics identified in the Attainment Targets. Some time may yet be needed to establish a broader curriculum in mathematics for low-attainers.

Curriculum content and assessment

Many teachers of mathematics in secondary schools welcome a National Curriculum which is not a comprehensive specification of the content to be taught but a core of basic requirements. The tendency to treat the National Curriculum as **the** curriculum is often associated with that of treating the National Curriculum as a set of objectives cast in the form of the Attainment Targets. In combination these can serve to impose severe limits on the possibility of delivering a broad curriculum at the same time as meeting assessment requirements and a diversity of needs in the classroom. A worrying possibility is that schools who adopt this position will necessarily limit the National Curriculum for pupils who experience difficulty in learning to Attainment Levels 3 and 4. The net result being the reduction of pupils' mathematical experience, including forms of language experience, to a focus on a small set of target statements which may come to have a tenuous relationship with any kind of meaningful and indeed valuable (or valued) experience. With low attainers, the National Curriculum requirements may make it difficult to acknowledge progress that individuals are making. Where progress is measurable within National Curriculum testing there would still appear to be cause for concern. In the most recent report (OFSTED, 1993b) Her Majesty's Chief Inspector reports that 'while progress across all four Key Stages was broadly in line with expectations, low achievers made disappointingly little progress throughout Key Stages 3 and 4'. There is certainly research evidence (Hart, 1981) to suggest that progress for low attainers through any learning hierarchies, particularly number and algebra, warrants consideration for assessment measures within levels, if any progress at all is to be acknowledged.

Since the Attainment Targets have been reduced both in number and in content, there is flexibility in planning ways to incorporate the National Curriculum demands into a school's mathematics curriculum.

Opportunities can be provided to allow pupils to work collaboratively as well as independently and to pursue topics of interest in some depth particularly where pupils with SEN may show capabilities in isolated aspects of the curriculum whilst their general attainment is low. The pressures of market forces in the form of aggregated scores on standardized tests and possibly appraisal exercises may sadly continue to make many mathematics departments and teachers feel constrained to abandon the struggle for flexibility for the sake of position in the market. Hopefully recent developments and reductions in the National Curriculum will allow schools to refocus their attention on the kinds of mathematical experiences which they wish to engage pupils in, rather than on attainments in isolation from methods and modes of communication.

Constraints are currently imposed by the system of Standardized Assessment Tests (SATs) being developed at Key Stage 3 and examinations at Key Stage 4. While careful thought may have been given to the content and contexts of the standardized tests, the mode of assessment as pencil and paper exercises under formal examination conditions is unlikely to enhance the performances of pupils who may be hampered by poor reading skills, limited concentration span and generally diffidence to assessment. But where pursuit of identifying attainment relates to assessment procedures by teachers in the classroom there are ways in which this can become a most constructive activity. *Diagnostic* assessment through which learning difficulties may be scrutinized and classified enables appropriate help and guidance to be provided. *Formative* assessment enables pupils and teachers to recognize positive achievements and negotiate in planning the next steps. Although the Task Group on Assessment and Testing (TGAT) (DES, 1988) commissioned to report on appropriate National Curriculum assessment, supported *summative* assessment only at the end of Key Stage 4, the reporting procedures that are being implemented show evidence that selective publication of results may distort the real position with regard to schools' achievements.

Record keeping and assessment are fundamental to the planning and monitoring of progress in mathematics and should not be confined to the procedures required by legislation. Her Majesty's Chief Inspector (OFSTED, 1993b) in the report on the implementation of the curricular requirements of the Education Reform Act reports, however, that 'about a tenth of the schools made good use of their records to plan for classes and individuals. However, in most of the schools there was some inflexible planning in that the work already planned would be done whatever the assessment evidence' (paragraph 39).

The purposes of assessment identified by Denvir (1988) include the use of assessment to improve the performance of pupils (and teachers!). Negotiation of goals for pupils that are related closely to the work undertaken and within the capabilities of individuals can result in substantial achievements as reported in the GAIM Project (1988) where graded assessment was based on negotiated progress through graded tasks. It is important not to forget assessment of attitudes to mathematics which will highlight the appropriateness of teaching approaches which affect motivation and may affect attainment. Again, the reality of the situation in classrooms currently does not appear to make effective use of pupil involvement in assessment: Her Majesty's Chief Inspector (OFSTED, 1993b) reports that although the marking of extended pieces of work was good, 'marking of other work rarely provided sufficient information for the pupils to know how they might improve their performance' and 'Pupils were not very involved in the assessment and recording of their attainment and tended to accept assessment and testing as procedures which were done to them'.

JUSTIFYING THE NEED FOR A BROADER CURRICULUM

It is sensible to look beyond statutory requirements in mathematics to examine the needs of pupils in school and their preparation for a role in society. When examining the needs of employment, the Cockcroft Committee reported that 'most jobs require only a limited range of mathematics' but acknowledged that 'widening of the mathematics curriculum ... has had a beneficial effect both in improving attitudes to mathematics and in laying the foundations for better understanding' (DES, 1982). But mathematics teaching may develop pupils' skills in logical thinking and planning that are an important part of all learning. Denvir *et al.*, in their study *Low Attainers in Mathematics: 5–16* (1982), note that 'Most jobs, at the least, require employees to plan logically and follow ordered procedures as, for example, in fault-finding and turning-on procedures for machinery'.

But mathematics can help people to lead a fuller and more satisfying life, for example, planning holidays and leisure activities, planning effective use of their income and engaging in games and sports that require strategies and scoring. Planning, calculating, recording and communicating are all skills that are integral to mathematics learning, accessible to all pupils and have applications beyond the classroom.

The Cockcroft Committee Report (DES, 1982) identified the last of these skills as the most powerful 'In our view the mathematics teacher has the task ... above all, of making each pupil aware that mathematics provides him with a powerful means of communication'. It is this aspect of communication that may help teachers to review their planning for mathematics so that 'what you know' is not the only measure of success but 'how you use what you know' may acknowledge achievement at all levels. Focus on communication in mathematics may also help planning for pupils who have a variety of learning difficulties. Such pupils may have differing sensory perception using their senses in ways that will lead to original and different contributions to activities and tasks. For example, hearing and sight impaired pupils can be successfully integrated in mainstream if teachers and peers learn to focus beyond their impairment. By focusing on the experiences that are denied disadvantaged pupils, teachers may be helped to address experiences that may be lacking in their classroom provision. Take for example the concept of a square held by a visually impaired student whose tactile experiences will be crucial to support an abstract description. If tactile experiences help visually impaired pupils, so they may help those whose sight is not impaired in learning. Practical activities that utilize a wide range of perceptual skills help all pupils develop a framework for conceptualizing mathematics and ultimately abstracting those concepts that are vital to mathematics understanding.

Hearing impaired pupils may be denied much of the richness in learning that discussion will provide but many pupils with learning difficulties benefit from visual and manipulative interactions with objects and images. In order not to make an impairment a handicap, additional experiences can be offered to compensate for those that may be missed. There must be a richness in activities planned to address a spectrum of special needs that are appropriate for the mathematics classroom.

Careful consideration of teaching approaches has implications for needs beyond those usually identified as SEN. Girls, for example may have a greater need than boys to develop understanding in mathematics through discussion (DES, 1989b) though they may be inhibited within the social structure of a mixed gender classroom. Again the idea of mathematics as a powerful means of communication may be encompassed.

Mathematics can be used to describe, to illustrate, to interpret, to predict and to explain. Many of these applications are found beyond arithmetic in work involving algebra and data handling. Mathematics is also an implicit part of the world we live in and a study of shape and space may grow from interactions with the environment that the pupils will know well. In order for learning to be meaningful for pupils with learning difficulties it should be relevant to their lives and pose questions and problems whose solutions the pupils are interested in finding out. That is not to say that all mathematics problems must be based on real-life scenarios for patterns and puzzles have widespread appeal and 'brain teasers' can provide substantial satisfaction when they are solved.

The aims of mathematics teaching identified in the HMI publication *Mathematics From 5 to 16* (1985) include developing 'awareness of the fascination of mathematics' and developing 'imagination, initiative and flexibility of mind' showing 'mathematics as a process, as a creative activity in which pupils can be fully involved, and not as an imposed body of knowledge immune to any change or development' (p. 4). This will be difficult to achieve without enthusiastic contributions from teachers who share the concept of mathematics as a creative activity and puts responsibility for special needs learners with mathematicians in school who may guide as well as be guided by the special needs support available. Classroom approaches that will enable development of these perceptions of mathematics, as well as nurturing a positive attitude to learning and application of mathematics, include appropriate practical work, problem solving and investigative approaches.

Appropriate practical work

Findings of the Assessment of Performance Unit (APU, 1989) reinforce what many teachers already know in suggesting that 'some pupils can demonstrate their knowledge more effectively in a practical interactive setting than is evident from their more formal written work' (p. 3). It is indicated that through a practical interactive approach, pupils will have the opportunity to engage in practical activities, showing what they can do and talking about it, giving them physical support to demonstrate their thinking rather than relying solely on verbal skills.

Practical work in mathematics is of three main kinds:

- that which enables pupils to understand mathematical concepts;
- practical work like measurement that is done with a purpose in mind;
- tasks that may be introduced or enhanced by a practical approach.

(from APU, 1989)

The first relates to the use of apparatus like bundles of sticks and real coins when working on place value. Such apparatus is usually available in primary school but resources are inadequate in most secondary schools (HMI, 1991). The resources for secondary school classrooms need not be costly and it may be beneficial to change from primary school experiences that could undermine pupils self image. Place-value relationships can be realized with 10-strips and 100-squares of card or paper which may be cut up with scissors to demonstrate decomposition in subtraction or accumulated to illustrate multiplication. Investment in five pounds worth of coins to show ones, tens and hundreds provides a wonderful incentive and a sense of responsibility within a structured environment.

> If teachers are to succeed in relating mathematics to the real
> world, worksheets constructed with money stamps like the one
> used with Danny, Mitesh and Jason (all seventeen-year-old
> students with considerable difficulty understanding money)
> involving images of one and two penny coins, must give way
> to experiences with coins that have texture and weight as well
> as real value! Collecting for a charity provided an opportunity
> to sort, count and calculate in a real and valuable context. The
> pupils were actively involved, highly-motivated and well-
> satisfied at their mathematical achievements at the end of a day
> of fund raising.

Practical activities in measuring can develop skills for life but can
also generate problems and investigations incorporating much
mathematics learning in the process. The GAIM project (1988) provides activities like designing a dining table for six people which incorporate ideas of shape, measuring and calculating in a real task whose
purpose can be appreciated and understood. Such extended tasks
enable teachers to support learning in a meaningful way and to assess
participants in their oral and written contributions.

Tasks can extend over several lessons and incorporate mathematical
concepts within a concrete setting or can be short tasks to support
concept development. Such practical approaches to mathematical
problems can be illustrated by the following lesson undertaken with
a small group of pupils within a class working on the topic of volume.

> Tom, Martin, Justin and Daniel were finding the number of
> individual cubes needed to construct a large cube whose sides
> were to be three units long. With a calculator they could not
> agree on the required total and embarked on the construction
> with cubes. Links between the construction and possible
> methods of calculating the total were discussed and the idea of
> volume was introduced by the teacher as the number of cubes
> in each layer taken three times or 'multiplied by 3'. Not only was
> it possible to discuss the number in each layer and the number
> of layers, leading to ideas of volume, but the problem could be
> extended to other shapes like cuboids or to finding out how
> many cubes cannot be seen or how many would have two faces
> painted if the outside of the cube were painted. Extensions to
> construct a $4 \times 4 \times 4$ cube involved further practical work and
> led to predictions and mathematical generalizations when the
> $5 \times 5 \times 5$ cube appeared too daunting to construct.

Whatever the outcome of a practical activity, the pupils are left with the experience and visual images that are vital to their conceptual framework for understanding mathematics and the discussion that provides language for communication and for thinking.

Practical mathematics may also relate to mathematics in the context of everyday problems and provide the opportunity to link theory to practice. The APU (1989) suggest decision making relating to shopping e.g. which product provides the best value for money, may form the basis for mathematical calculations and discussions. Here, the mathematical working will have meaning for pupils who may even be interested in the outcome of such calculations. It is also suggested that probability and data handling provide appropriate practical tasks with opportunities for pupils to predict and generalize their findings as well as discussing and analysing their observations. The use of modern technology, in particular calculators and computers, may be introduced to support pupils with SEN in structuring their explorations. Using spread sheets or data handling packages to organize findings and to present results in a variety of formats not only provides opportunities for hands on experiences but motivates discussion and collaborative learning. A useful introduction to the use of spreadsheets is to be found in the appendix to the Mathematical Association Report *Computers in the Mathematics Curriculum* (1992). This report identifies many roles for the computer in the classroom and is recommended as a general guide for mathematics and special needs teachers who would like to find out more. The use of calculators will be discussed in the next chapter.

HMI (1985) highlight the importance of practical work which enables pupils to understand mathematical concepts and identify particularly the role of structural apparatus and experiences with water and containers in developing the concepts of volume and capacity. Too often it is seen to be the role of primary school teachers to undertake this type of practical activity. For pupils with SEN, such practical experiences need to be revisited where concepts are insecure. But all secondary pupils should have access to materials to support abstract relationships in mathematics. HMI note that:

> without sufficient practical experience the pupils are unable to relate abstract mathematical concepts to any form of reality. *All pupils benefit from appropriate practical work of this kind* whatever their age and ability. (p. 39)

Practical activities may generate opportunities for pupils to develop language and mathematical reasoning as required in the first Attainment Target 'Using and Applying Mathematics' through discussion and collaborative decision making. There is also a requirement for pupils to 'select and use the appropriate mathematics and materials to help solve problems' (SCAA, 1994, p. 8). This signals the central role of problem solving in mathematics and the expectation that practical activities will be available in the mathematics classroom.

Problem solving

> The ability to solve problems is at the heart of mathematics.
>> (Cockcroft Report, DES, 1982, para. 249)

The word 'problem' has negative connotations that can affect pupils self-perception if they have had unsuccessful experiences in their lives. To solve problems may be at the heart of mathematics but it involves complex skills that interact and require procedural management that needs teacher encouragement and support if pupils with learning difficulties are to be successful. But this approach is rewarded by pupils becoming more involved in their mathematical learning and surpassing teacher expectations of their work.

Reporting on the Low Attainers in Mathematics Project (LAMP 1983–6) and its successor the Raising Achievements in Mathematics Project (RAMP 1986–9) Trickett and Sulke (1988) identify 'better ability and willingness to question, to transfer and apply their mathematics and to sort out even quite difficult problems' as some of the benefits of a problem solving approach.

Teachers should first identify appropriate problems, acknowledging the value of the open-ended kind where different outcomes are possible and the merits of different solutions may be discussed. Such mathematical problems may be found in textbooks, reference books, professional journals, games and puzzles as well as in other subjects and in home life and employment. But the greatest motivation arises when the problems are posed by the pupils themselves. Teachers can exploit the opportunities that arise in classroom interactions and negotiate tasks that will engage the pupils in questions and solutions they can identify with. Real problems for pupils may not be particular to special needs learners and may involve such subjects as the inadequacy of locker facilities for their belongings or inappropriate bicycle storage or the timeless problem of not having enough money or free time. All of these can provide fruitful mathematical experiences. Take for example the dimensions, costs and siting of lockers which may be related to their use in school and the 'flow' of users in any day. Questionnaires may be constructed to collect data relating to pupils use of lockers and their views on appropriate siting. Catalogues can be studied to investigate the dimensions and costing of different options and reports prepared for submission to school management. Such investigations will generate a lot of mathematical working, may help identify solutions to problems and may have positive benefits for the school environment generally. (It is worth stressing to pupils that mathematical solutions to problems have often to be judged by criteria of a non-mathematical nature, for example political, social or moral constraints that may be involved.)

According to Randall and Lester (1982) good problem-solving behaviour is often not fostered by teachers who are inclined to demonstrate correct moves discouraging pupils' efforts that may appear to be misdirected or inefficient. Appropriate teacher actions are suggested in their book *Teaching Problem Solving* which includes the purposes and uses of teacher actions and ways to adjust teacher actions to meet the needs of both high and low achievers. Problem solving can only be real when the pupils take responsibility for their own mathematical thinking and is perhaps typified when the role of the teacher changes from one of responsibility for what the pupils do and learn to one of being a resource for their learning. The role of the teacher is to provide a structured framework within which the pupils may be guided to follow their own lines of enquiry and gain confidence in their abilities to tackle problems both individually and in collaboration with others.

'Pupils will require a great deal of discussion and oral work before even very simple problems can be tackled in written form' (Cockcroft Report, DES, 1982, para. 249). The introduction and negotiation of problems may provide the first stage in which responsibility and control can be seen by the pupils to be in their hands. When selecting problems for use in the classrooms, teachers need to judge their appropriateness against a number of criteria:

It must be accessible to everyone at the start.
It needs to allow further challenges and be extendible.
It should invite pupils to make decisions.
It should involve pupils in speculating, hypothesis making and testing, proving or explaining, reflecting, interpreting.
It should not restrict pupils from searching in other directions.
It should promote discussion and communication.
It should encourage originality/invention.
It should encourage 'what if' and 'what if not' questions.
It should have an element of surprise.
It should be enjoyable.

(Trickett and Sulke, 1988, p. 115)

Teachers need also to analyse their role in the pupils problem solving. In her book *Thinking Things Through: Problem Solving in Mathematics*, Burton (1984) identifies four phases of activity in problem solving referred to as Entry, Attack, Review and Extension and then analyses the organization of questions, procedures and skills that are the necessary elements of such problem solving. These are illuminated through a number of examples with associated pupils' work.

Analysis of the purposes of a problem solving approach and the different stages that may be involved is helpful though the thirty problems proposed in the book, each accompanied by notes for the teacher and indications of the mathematics involved, may need considerable modification to make them accessible to all pupils.

The report on the Low Attainers in Mathematics Project (LAMP) and the Raising Achievements in Mathematics Project (RAMP) includes teachers' accounts of the way problem solving led them to revise their ideas about mathematics and change their classroom methods:

> Remarkable results have been achieved with pupils from mainstream and special schools when the teaching of mathematics has been opened up in order to allow pupils to find their own strategies and solution to problems.
>
> (from Ahmed, 1989)

These findings contrast with those of Hofmeister who summarized some research on problem solving and provides a set of implications for instruction in mathematics:

1. Domain specific, problem solving skill can and should be taught.
2. Some generalization of problem solving skills should be planned for and systematically taught.
3. It may be unreasonable to expect the majority of problem solving strategies in one domain to transfer to another domain.
4. The development of problem solving skills will require a considerable investment in explicitly taught strategies and practice.
5. The teaching of problem solving strategies should be integrated with the teaching of other content in the domain such as computational and factual knowledge.

(from Hofmeister, 1989)

To resolve what appears to be contradictory evidence about the extent to which problem solving must be taught and supported or pupils left to their own devices, it is necessary to analyse further the procedures involved. Teachers can then judge appropriate intervention which will vary with individual pupils in order to maximize challenge and motivation and avoid discouragement through prolonged frustration.

Problem solving procedures related specifically to pupils with learning difficulties involving particularly work on number problems may be found in an article by Williams who elaborates on six stages of number problem solving with practical implication for each stage:

STAGE 1.   Identifying mathematics within the problem

Practical implications

• At every stage, from first school onwards, a substantial proportion of mathematical activity should be problem based whereby pupils are expected to create their own formulations from data derived from a wide variety of situations.

• At every stage, the demands made by problems will be commensurate with the conceptual and ability level of the pupil.

STAGE 2. Identifying relevant elements within the problem

Practical implications

• The problems presented must be real, or, if simulation is necessary, credible to the pupils and within their experience. No taps filling baths!

• Identification of relevant data is rendered more likely if pupils work in pairs or small groups in which discussion is encouraged. Motivation might be high enough to engender an argument! The dynamics of group-formation merit careful consideration.

• Structural and other concrete apparatus should be freely available to form analogues of the reality situation, if and when required.

STAGE 3. Determining the appropriate mathematical process

Practical implications

• The key to this stage is the provision of frequent opportunities for pupils to experiment in the application of the four basic processes to self-obtained data on a discussion basis.

• Make use of actual materials, models, structural apparatus and blackboard diagrams.

• Avoid repetitive examples, based on one particular process, in characteristic text book style. This lessens the need for conceptualization of the problem as a whole.

STAGE 4. Estimating the answer

Practical implications

• It should be the *unvarying* practice both for arithmetic calculations and problems for pupils to be required to make a preliminary estimate of the expected answer.

• Encourage pupils to justify their estimates to each other.

STAGE 5. Working out the calculations

Practical implications

• Though the calculations asked of pupils will normally derive from practical situations, reinforcement of skills and processes may be necessary by giving further examples.

• A relational approach to calculations, essential to problem solving, will differentiate between concept formation, skill and process development and the acquisition of mathematical knowledge.

• The obtained answer will be checked against the estimate obtained at stage 4.

• In instances where there is a discrepancy between the estimate and the obtained answer, pupils themselves should be encouraged to identify the origin and nature of the error with difficulties referred first to a partner before the teacher is brought into the discussion.

• Persistent errors in calculation should be classified as a basis for teaching.

STAGE 6. Taking the answer back to the problem

Practical implications

• Having placed the answer within the context of the original problem, the pupil(s) consider what action is appropriate.

• Are the outcomes sufficiently significant to merit a wider audience? Depending on the scale of the problem this may vary on the scale of discussion with a partner, to letter writing, making posters, giving lectures or any other means of dissemination. Mathematics is exciting so let's share the excitement!

• Consider with the pupil(s) possible extensions of the problem. Such discussions will be strongly influenced by the degree of motivation engendered by the original problem and the impact of its outcomes. Decisions on this point call for particular sensitivity on the teacher's part.

(from Williams, 1985)

It is not suggested that every problem requires detailed attention at all stages but reflections and interactions of the type suggested will generate an atmosphere for learning in which individual's contributions are valued within pupil centred and task centred activities.

Problem solving can provide a rich environment from which much learning in mathematics may be achieved. HMI (1991), however, note the problem solving in many classrooms is tackled through a 'bolt on' approach with a series of activities done after the content has been learned – typically in texts with pages of 'problems' at the end of chapters giving pupils the impression that mathematics exists to be applied to problems (if you know how to do that) rather than mathematics arising out of the problems to be solved.

Further evidence relating to the use of problem solving in social interactions is provided by Schoenfeld (1985) and will be discussed later in this chapter.

Games in the mathematics classroom

Among the most appealing task-centred activities used in the secondary classroom can be mathematical games. Games have often been regarded as 'time-fillers' or end of term activities but may now be found integrated into many school maths schemes. So powerful is the environment created through a game that National Curriculum Assessment may be found incorporating games to enable assessment against specific criteria. In his review of the research into the use of games, Paul Ernest presents an argument for the effectiveness of games in teaching mathematics and claims that games teach mathematics effectively in four ways:

- by providing reinforcement and practice
- by providing motivation
- by helping the acquisition and development of concepts
- by developing problem solving strategies.

(from Ernest, 1986)

Within a game, routine calculations may be repeated many times in a non-threatening environment where motivation persists through interactive play. Many games encourage the development of a winning strategy but can give equal chances to all players where there is also an element of chance. The best games to encourage mathematical learning are those in which the structure and rules are based on mathematical ideas and winning the game will depend on understanding those ideas. Janet Ainley gives as examples the well-known games of Fizz-Buzz and Nim. In her chapter 'Playing Games and Real Mathematics' she identifies the ways games can help pupils learn mathematics and identifies some of the skills that may be developed through games:

- prediction
- conjecturing
- generalizing
- checking and justifying.

(from Ainley, 1988)

Even those who find it impossible not to cheat may generate some quite sophisticated strategies to engineer winning. This is not to be condoned but indicates that mathematical learning can take place in what appear to be adverse circumstances.

The game of 'Grabs' involves individual pupils in grabbing a handful of pegs and arranging them on a peg board in pairs. If they have a precise number of pairs, they score this number, if they grabbed an odd number of pegs they score nothing. The same collection of pegs is now reorganized into threes and the same scoring system applies: if the number of threes is exact, they score that number, otherwise they score nothing. Play continues until the pegs have been resorted into fours and fives. Ten further points are scored if they can estimate the exact number of pegs they grabbed.

Rob (12.5) scored 11 when he sorted his pegs into twos and claimed a score of 7 when sorting into threes. Caught out by the teacher who knew immediately he had conveniently 'lost' a peg, he puzzled about how this was done. As he continued to play, he worked hard to understand the relationship between the numbers and successfully analysed what was going on. Tina (11.9) and Anna (12.3) opted to take small grabs that were easy to organize on the peg board but Jim (11.10) grabbed the biggest handful he could manage and began to use grouping to count his large collections. In the group of four there was little co-operation or interactive discussion during the lesson but by the next session when the game was played two of the others also had a good idea of what relationships were involved in the game.

Practical advice on the selection and classroom organization for playing games to encourage mathematics learning can be found in David Kirby's *Games in the Teaching of Mathematics*. He classifies games into different types and provides photocopy masters for use in the classroom. His intention in compiling this collection was to 'illustrate ways in which games can be given a higher profile' and his aims:

1. To consider ways of categorizing games.
2. To outline techniques for adapting and inventing games.
3. To focus particularly on ways of using games as a means of generating mathematical activity.
4. To suggest ideas for making the learning of traditional topics fun and exciting.
5. To provide an all-round resource for teachers and student teachers of mathematics.

(from Kirby, 1992)

All these are well met in this valuable publication.

Not least among the benefits of problem solving and using games in the mathematics classroom are those offered to teachers who may find pupils' motivation improved, find increased opportunities for observing pupils' thinking strategies and opportunities for interactions that are easy and more natural.

SOCIAL INTERACTION

Among the studies concerning the social interactions of pupils with special educational needs those concerning the learning of mathematics provide important discussion. Interactions with peers as well as with teachers provide valuable opportunities for pupils to share understandings and engage in verbalization of thought processes that will enhance learning. Interactions may take different forms and teacher planning should have clear objectives for the structuring of lessons.

Teaching can involve setting up and 'managing' group and class discussions.

Year 7 'bottom set' were given a list of sums to consider – not to solve! – they were asked to work as groups to decide which was the most difficult sum and which was the easiest and then rank them in order of difficulty.

This generated a lot of discussion and negotiation with different solution strategies being compared as implicit stages in the pupil's arguments. Comparing the problem $18 + 7 =$ to the problem $6000 + 6 =$ depended on confidence with large numbers and understanding of the place value. Mark (12.7) was confident that 'six thousand add six just means the same as six thousand and six' while Sam (12.2) could calculate $18 + 7$ by counting on his fingers so found this sum 'much easier'.

This activity also required reflection on what the question was asking, for example, $36 \div 7 =$ provoked much discussion about whether it was 'fair to have one left over'.

Discussion revealed misconceptions, for example, $29 \div 5 =$ was 'impossible because 29 is not in the 5 times table' or involved 'remainder 1' because it was one away from 30. After involving herself with various groups, the teacher asked the different groups to report their ranking of the problems and 'managed' a whole class discussion to compare the opinions of the different groups.

Group work

Problem solving and games provide opportunities for group work in mathematics with inherent advantages. In the Assessment of Performance (APU) booklet *Communicating Mathematical Ideas* the efficacy of a practical interactive approach is outlined with advice on setting up group situations and developing mathematical oracy. Among the advantages of using group work are listed the following:

  (i) It gives pupils opportunity to talk to other pupils about mathematics.
 (ii) Pupils often spark ideas off one another.
(iii) Pupils have been known to do better at individual work when they have experienced group work.
 (iv) Pupils often find it easier to see what other pupils have difficulty in understanding and can sometimes explain more clearly than can the teacher.
  (v) Pupils may find it easier to express their difficulties to people of their own age rather than the teacher.
 (vi) Pupils are often more motivated and involved than they normally are in mathematics lessons.
(vii) Some teachers felt that pupils working on their own often kept to a very narrow channel, whereas in groups pupils can pool ideas.

(from APU, 1989)

Support for small group work is also found in Schoenfeld who suggests that it promotes the process of learning in four ways:

  (i) It provides opportunities for teacher assessment.
 (ii) Group decision making facilitates the articulation of knowledge and reasoning.
(iii) Students receive practice in collaboration.
 (iv) Insecure students are able to watch more capable peers struggle.

(from Schoenfeld, 1985)

Co-operative learning

High reliance on peer group discussion to promote mathematics learning comes in the form of co-operative learning. There have been many attempts to promote co-operative learning in the mathematics classrooms of mainstream schools (e.g. Mevarech, 1985). These developments sometimes tacitly and sometimes explicitly reflect the influence of social views in developmental psychology and such initiatives may be viewed as a response to or a reaction to the overly individualistic constructivist paradigm derived from Piagetian studies. There have also been a number of attempts to co-operative learning approaches with pupils with special needs (e.g. Ashman and Elkins, 1990; Johnson and Johnson, 1986) and specifically in mathematics for pupils with special needs (e.g. Tateyama-Sniezek, 1990).

However as Wood (1988) notes whilst there are a number of laboratory-style experimental studies that suggest that co-operative learning may help facilitate learning the case for beneficial effects in the classroom remains not proven. Citing the work of Bennett *et al.* (1984) he argues that observations of classroom behaviour indicate that positive effects found in experiments are rarely repeated in the classroom. Wood does not 'close the door' on co-operative problem solving but suggests that much more needs to be understood about matching pupils, selecting tasks and managing groups before confidence can be placed in this 'potentially invaluable learning and teaching resource in the classroom'.

In the absence of a high level of confidence in the form of co-operative learning that arises in classrooms as a way of making progress, it would seem that the areas of curriculum content and pedagogic process involving the *teacher* deserve attention.

Reciprocal teaching

Reciprocal teaching is a term used by Palincsar and Brown (1988) and Gilroy and Moore (1988) to refer to an innovative tutoring strategy whereby teachers and students assume the role of 'the teacher'. The adult or student 'teacher model' aids learners in the internalization of similar comprehension strategies. The teacher or more capable peer structures the students' learning through four strategies:

1. Summarizing: identifying and paraphrasing the main idea in the text.
2. Question-Generating: self-questioning about the type of information that is generally tapped on tests of comprehension and recall.
3. Clarifying: discerning when there has been a breakdown in comprehension and taking the necessary action to restore meaning (e.g., reading ahead, rereading, asking for assistance).
4. Predicting: hypothesizing what the structure and content of the text suggest will be presented next.

(from Palincsar, 1986)

There have been a number of recent attempts, inspired by Vygotskian theory, to introduce forms of reciprocal teaching that are designed to be responsive to the instructional needs of the individual, (Palincsar and Brown, 1984; Daniels, 1988). These encourage the teacher to engage in pedagogic dialogues which are not delimited by inflexible views about curriculum progression. The instructional needs of pupils, many of whom may have communication difficulties, are destined to be difficult to discern. A form of pedagogy which enables the teacher to learn about the child's instructional needs is required. Importantly a flexible view of curriculum sequence must be retained.

This type of approach may be thought of as one in which pupils are required to externalize their self-regulatory practices in order to open them to instruction and development. Palincsar and Brown (1988) achieved this in the context of acting out problem solving with pupils. This approach has also been used by Schoenfeld who reports teaching in which the teacher thought aloud as mathematical problems were being solved. By drawing attention to the problem solving procedures being used he was providing a model for his undergraduate students to use in their own problem solving processes:

> What do you do when you have a problem like this? I have no general procedure for finding the roots of a polynomial, much less for comparing the two roots of them. Probably the best thing to do for the time being is to look at some simple examples and hope I can develop some intuition for them. Instead of looking at a pair of arbitrary polynomials, maybe I should look at a pair of quadratics: at least I can solve those. Now what happens if . . .
>
> (from Schoenfeld, 1985)

In this way Schoenfeld was making visible that which was hidden. Far too often novice learners get the wrong idea about the ways that experts perform tasks. For example many pupils in schools seem to have little understanding of the way their teachers write. The process of drafting and sculpting text is lost and replaced by the mistaken idea that one starts an essay at the beginning and finishes at the end with no crossing out or frustration at getting stuck. Similar perceptions of adults' and more able peers' abilities in mathematical problem solving may mask 'natural' procedures and inhibit learners in their apparently 'clumsy' efforts. In his analysis of problem solving behaviours, Schoenfeld introduces classifications using the terms 'beliefs', 'control', 'heuristics' and 'resources' which could be of interest to teachers of all pupils including those with SEN.

Pupils may also co-operate with teachers or more able peers in an activity that is more complex than they can understand when working on their own. In reciprocal teaching the child works with the teacher's understanding without necessarily being directly taught. Newman, Griffin and Cole provide an important account of the process of social mediation in learning to divide. They studied division because it provides a clear example of learning in which responsibility is transferred from teacher to learner and then back from learner to teacher in a series of cycles of increasing understanding and learner control.

> The problem facing the student can be phrased as follows: the student must acquire the concept, 'gazinta' (goes into). At the outset, the child is confronted with the confusing request to say how many times '5 gazinta 27'. Before this time in the arithmetic curriculum, the child has worked on 'number facts', viz., 'five 5s are 25; five 6s are 30' and only 'three 9s' or 'nine 3s' are 27. So, how can 5 'go into' 27? Five can 'go into' 25 or 30; but only 3 or 9 can 'go into' 27! Expert skill in carrying out the procedure actually calls for an initial estimate of the quotient, which is then checked and adjusted in the subsequent steps . . . the initial step of estimating is a very difficult thing to explain to the novice who does not yet know what it is that one is attempting to estimate!
>
> (from Newman *et al.*, 1989)

Another such example of evolving responsibilities is outlined in Kibel's account of her interactions involving fourteen-year-old Alex. Using structured apparatus, she used a game situation to observe Alex's developing use of language to help his understanding of subtraction. Each starting with a hundred square Dienes block on a board, the idea was to 'shrink' the square by throwing a dice and taking away the number of cubes thrown:

> Alex and I took a long time working our way down from 100. It became much too easy, and so to make the game more fun we began closing our eyes as we manipulated the blocks and described what we were doing. Next, we tried describing the whole process, eyes shut, without touching the blocks at all. This proved surprisingly hard for Alex. The temptation to open his eyes and handle the blocks was very strong. He could not sustain the language on its own. But eventually, given time and practice, the verbal explanations became surprisingly easy and the blocks almost superfluous. At this point we transferred to the formal written algorithm. The transition was swift and trouble-free. Alex left that afternoon feeling that we had an amusing time, nothing more.
>
> But the effect was dramatic. Alex was 14. He had never understood how to do subtraction when this involved 'borrowing'. He regularly took the lowest number from the highest, regardless ... − and he regularly got his answers wrong! Some time later, he called round and proudly announced, 'I can do those take-aways. They're easy. We've been doing them at school this week and I got them all right. No problem! They're *ace*, they are'.
>
> ... A month later he could still do them and to my knowledge he has not forgotten to this day.
>
> (from Kibel, 1992)

Both of the above encounters illustrate the idea that there are processes in learning which must properly be characterized as *interpsychological* – arising from the interaction between people. The issue here is the transfer of control or regulation of task-related activities from teacher to learner. The teacher and child start out doing the task together. For example the teacher may initially take the major part of the responsibility for executing the task and the child may play a relatively small part. The teacher's intention will be to gradually transfer control of progress in task completion to the learner.

ACTIVE PARTICIPATION

Inspection of current reviews of the practice of mathematics education both in the UK and the USA suggests something of a gap between theory and practice especially for pupils with SEN. Following the European move towards autonomy and independent learning referred to in Chapter 1 the work of Parmar and Cawley (1991) suggests that appropriate changes in instructional procedures can result in important affective outcomes. They bemoan the extent to which the active construction of mathematical meaning on the part of pupils, described in the USA as having mild mental handicaps, is ignored:

> The quality of education for special education students is seriously wanting. We are concerned with the extent to which the passive learning attributes ascribed to pupils with mild handicaps are in fact the result of the instruction they receive. (p. 25)

Here a constructivist analysis is used to highlight the dangers of a transmission-based pedagogy. In brief the pupils are rendered passive by the form of instruction they receive.

Parmar and Cawley made use of a Japanese instructional procedure. Their intention was to move away from what they claim is the all too familiar practice in American classrooms of fostering passive rote responding to work sheets with little time for discussion and analysis. The typical procedure being a presentation of information, followed by a group session of working through a few examples, followed by individual worksheets of large numbers of related problems. They suggest that 'a common format of a Japanese mathematics lesson is for the teacher to assign a small number of items (about four to six) that can be completed rather rapidly. Once the students are finished, the students and the teacher spend the remainder of the period discussing and analysing these few problems' (ibid., p. 24). Parmar and Cawley supplemented the Japanese procedure by requiring pupils to generate their own practice materials. Arguing that such activities help to discourage the negative feelings of helplessness engendered by passive procedures, they suggest that co-operative discussion of a small number of problems results in more autonomous and confident learners. Further reading relating to a large-scale observational comparative study on American, Japanese and Taiwanese classrooms pointing out differences in expectations and classroom behaviours is to found in Stigler and Perry *Mathematics Learning in Chinese, Japanese and American Classrooms* (1990).

Baroody and Hume (1991) also refer to Japanese pedagogy and suggest a number of ways to improve how mathematics is taught:

- Focus on understanding
- Encourage purposeful learning
- Foster informal knowledge
- Link formal instruction to informal knowledge
- Encourage reflection and discussion. (pp. 55–6)

They argue that their version of Socratic teaching enables teachers to meet these demands. In this setting the teacher asks a question or sets a problem and through sensitive questioning helps the learner to construct their own understanding of the problem.

GENERAL TEACHING IMPLICATIONS

A large part of the plea for reform issued by Parmar and Cawley, and Baroody and Hume is with respect to raising teacher expectation/belief in the creative capacity of pupils with learning difficulties. This is an issue which is given some depth of treatment in Good and Brophy (1984) *Looking in Classrooms.* Arguably this is the same theme explored by Ahmed (1989) when he discusses the 'spiritual violence' committed against pupils referred to as low attainers in schools. He suggests that too much of the practice of mathematics teaching may be seen to:

1. Focus the cause of failure on the pupil.
2. Believe that a good staff pupil ratio is the answer to slow learning.
3. Lower pupil expectations.
4. Lower teacher expectations.
5. Lower parent expectations.
6. Use methods of teaching which lead to fear of failure. (p. 69)

In the course of the DES funded RAMP and LAMP projects, directed by Ahmed, teachers and pupils were seen to be engaged in endless repetition of basic arithmetic rules. The project teams produced evidence that significant improvements could be achieved if the underlying negative image of the pupil could be changed.

He employs the ironic device of citing a description of a gifted child and suggesting that this could also be appropriately applied in the case of many a 'low-attaining pupil':

1. Intellectual curiosity.
2. Learns easily and readily.
3. Have a broad range of interests.
4. Have a broad attention span that enables them to concentrate on, and persevere in solving problems and pursuing interests.
5. Have ability to do effective work independently.
6. Exhibit keen powers of observation.
7. Show initiative and originality in intellectual work.
8. Show alertness and quick responses to new ideas.
9. Possess unusual imagination.

(Ibid., p. 72)

SUMMARY

In this chapter we have proposed the case for a broad curriculum in mathematics that is not constrained by the requirements of the National Curriculum but extends to incorporate the aims of mathematics teaching identified in the HMI (1985) publication *Mathematics from 5–16* and makes mathematics learning a meaningful and enjoyable experience for all pupils.

We acknowledge the central role of problem solving and have documented studies demonstrating the effectiveness of a problem solving approach for pupils with SEN. We also identify practical activities and games as a means of promoting discussion and social interaction to involve the pupils in their own learning, to establish some ownership for the mathematics and to encourage recognition that there are applications of this learning in the 'real' world beyond school.

The way to raise attainment in mathematics for low-achieving pupils involves mathematics and special needs teachers moving through a cycle of planning, implementing and evaluating a wide range of tasks providing breadth and balance of content and a variety of teaching and learning approaches. A range of open and investigational tasks can be introduced alongside more specifically targeted activities so that confidence and interest may be nurtured in an environment that involves pupils in choice and decision making. Pupils contributions, however misguided, can be valued by teachers and peers who will become involved jointly in a process of discussion and negotiation. A lone voice may be airing misconceptions that are inhibiting understanding of fundamental concepts. As teachers and pupils question and explain to each other, mathematical thinking will develop, together with the communication skills that are vital for a role in society today.

5

Pupils' ways of working

Having discussed classroom approaches that may develop those skills associated with mathematical thinking and using mathematics, this chapter will consider the pupils' roles in their own learning. There is a considerable literature concerning research into pupils' ways of working in mathematics and this chapter will explore the relevance of such research to pupils with learning difficulties. If the teacher is to become a 'facilitator' for learning rather than a deliverer of knowledge, it is essential to be aware of pupils' ways of working at mathematical tasks. The teacher is then able to build on the understandings the pupil possesses rather than trying to impose more information on a cognitive framework that may be insecure or organized in a manner that does not accord with a way of understanding a problem that is implicit in the instruction.

PUPILS' UNDERSTANDING

Any experienced teacher will realize that there may be a considerable gap between what pupils can do and what they understand. Skemp (1976) distinguished between the type of rote learning ('instrumental understanding') that enables pupils to find the correct solutions to problems without understanding why the procedures work and meaningful learning ('procedural understanding') with which the pupil not only knows what to do but also why. He concludes that although it may be easier to teach for 'instrumental understanding' and get quick results in the short term, it is harder for pupils to remember and may prove to be quite demotivating if 'procedural understanding' is not an outcome. When progress in learning is slow, it is tempting to teach specific procedures in the anticipation that understanding will come later. It is therefore not uncommon to find pupils in the secondary school with confused memories of a number of procedures that they have encountered, half remembered and never clearly understood.

Assessing pupils' understanding is not straightforward when many assessment procedures measure skills in taught processes rather than mathematical understanding. The research programme 'Concepts in Secondary Mathematics and Science' (CSMS 1974-9) set out to assess pupils' understanding over a range of eleven mathematical topics including number, algebra, graphs and transformation geometry. The project tested extensively in the UK and its findings, published in Hart's *Children's Understanding of Mathematics: 11–16* (1981), have had impact on classroom practices and on curriculum development. As well as establishing the types of mathematical tasks pupils are actually able to solve, these findings also reveal fundamental misconceptions. Apparently straightforward tasks such as identifying the correct arithmetic operation to use to solve a word problem or 'reading' information from simple graphs prove to be the source of much confusion. In the more recent report *The Implementation of the Curricular Requirements of the Education Reform Act: Mathematics– Key Stages 1, 2, 3 and 4, the Fourth Year 1992–93* (OFSTED, 1993b), Her Majesty's Chief Inspector reports that '[pupils] found it difficult to answer questions in context where they had to decide which operation (for example, multiplication or division) to use. No significant improvement was noted in this important aspect of number work' (p. 6). Costello (1991) indicates generally how the CSMS project has influenced curriculum development and how 'the treatment of some topic areas has provided a framework within which strategies for teaching, learning and doing mathematics can be described and interpreted'. The study generally increased awareness of just how difficult school mathematics is for some pupils.

For many pupils, learning difficulties originate with the standard procedures of arithmetic which present a formidable hurdle beyond which they may never progress. They may be confident with real objects in front of them but unable to relate to the abstract symbols and language that are associated with the formalization of arithmetic. Sometimes geometric ideas are less daunting and enable greater success in mathematical attainment as well as practical preparation for life. For low-attaining pupils there appear to be two major problems: how to develop mathematics beyond the content of arithmetic that currently occupies a disproportionate amount of their school maths lessons and how to ensure that arithmetic teaching enables these young people to develop skills in thinking and communicating required in mathematics and beyond.

NUMBER SKILLS

Formally taught written algorithms in arithmetic have little value for pupils who do not understand the procedures that are involved and cannot apply them to real life problems. As suggested above, memorizing procedures often leads to short-term retention and confusion on recall. So how can teachers develop number understanding and sound problem solving skills? A move away from standardized solution procedures towards the development of personal strategies will enable teachers to encourage all attempts at solutions and to work with the pupils towards refinements that will reveal misconceptions and improve success rates, ultimately generating more efficient procedures.

> In order to progress through the (National Curriculum) levels, pupils . . . must be encouraged and helped to develop *their own* methods for doing calculations . . . What is important is that all pupils are encouraged to develop their range of skills, make sensible decisions about how to tackle calculations and be confident in the use of methods both within mathematics and in other contexts.
>
> (DES, 1989b)

If we can develop in pupils a 'feel for number' that incorporates an ability to judge the reasonableness of answers and to approximate solutions where appropriate and gets away from the mindless application of half-forgotten rules, this number sense will provide the basis for tackling the problems that will arise in the workplace and home. This number sense must include familiarity with calculators which will provide confidence and efficiency if used in conjunction with established number sense. HMCI reports:

> Although there has been a slight increase in mental work, insufficient attention continued to paid to approximation and estimation, to mental and calculator skills, to the development of understanding or to the use of the knowledge and skills in a variety of contexts . . . Too many of the pupils, however, especially low attainers, lacked the 'feel for number' and confidence necessary to use and apply the skills in the future.
>
> (OFSTED, 1993b, p. 6)

CALCULATORS

The Cockcroft Report (DES, 1982) identified the central place of mental calculations in mathematics. This has been reinforced by HMCI (OFSTED, 1993b) and needs to be reflected in appropriate teaching approaches that encourage mental methods as a 'first resort' when a calculation is needed. This must be balanced with methods that encourage calculator explorations and the development of pencil and paper methods as appropriate to the problem situation.

Despite widespread reliance on calculators in the workplace and in personal life, many people still fear that young people who are allowed to use calculators will not develop fluency in computation and their ability to recall basic number facts may be weakened. Extensive studies in the USA indicate strongly that this is not the case and the CAN (Calculator-Aware Number) Project (1985–89) suggests that the opposite may be true with pupils' number understanding strengthened and extended through their access to calculators. Hembree (1992) presents a useful overview of research in the USA on the introduction of calculators and refers to the positive effects on low-attainers confidence in handling arithmetic and in successful problem solving.

As well as being a positive motivator calculators will enable and encourage exploration of numbers with instant access to correct answers in a non-threatening environment. Inputting $6 \times 7 = \ldots$ on a calculator will always generate the response 42 where pencil and paper or the use of apparatus may lead to close approximations: the pupil who has difficulty calculating 6×7 is inevitably the one who miscounts cubes or forgets fundamental steps in an algorithmic procedure. Calculators not only take the labour out of calculations, releasing time for thinking about the mathematics and methodologies involved in finding solutions but also present the most important piece of mathematical equipment for adult life.

Shuard reporting on the Calculator-Aware Number Curriculum (CAN) Project notes that it has become clear that a calculator 'does not at once transform a low-attaining pupil's understanding of mathematics, because a calculator only helps with the actual calculation – it does not tell the operator which keys to press to solve a particular problem. However, a calculator may transform the confidence of a low-attaining pupil':

> Using a calculator can do much more than merely assisting with calculation. It gives another way in which children can explore numbers for themselves, and find out how they work. It is impossible to stop children 'playing' with their calculators, and a calculator is the first 'toy' that embodies the number system, and that allows children to explore numbers as they 'play'. The CAN children have explored large numbers, negative numbers and decimals at a much earlier stage than would be expected in a conventional curriculum – and they have done this of their own initiative, not because the teacher insisted on it. Of course, the more able and confident children explore much further, but all undertake exploration, and the low-attaining children explore numbers at the level at which that exploration will help them.
>
> (from Shuard, 1991)

Reports of the Shell/Leicestershire primary schools project (Moore, 1985) also suggest very positive response and suggest that calculators have potential as a teaching and learning aid for pupils with learning difficulties in the following ways:

(i) Calculators promote discussion and reveal misconceptions.
(ii) Calculators can help focus pupil's attention and increase concentration span.
(iii) Calculators can help pupils gain confidence and can promote enjoyment of mathematics activities.
(iv) Calculators can help in the implementation of the greater variety of kinds of maths lessons considered essential for the teaching of mathematics at all levels (Cockcroft, 1982). In particular, they allow more balance between acquiring skills and using them in meaningful ways.

Non-Statutory Guidance (DES, 1989b) for the National Curriculum advises that calculators:

> provide a fast and efficient means of calculation, liberating pupils and teachers from excessive concentration on pencil and paper methods. By increasing the options available to pupils, by enabling more ambitious exploration of numbers to be undertaken, and by saving time in making calculations, calculators offer an opportunity to increase standards of attainment. (E5)

Calculators may also present the important link for low-attaining pupils between real problems and the symbolic arithmetic involved. Using a calculator can only become efficient if the most appropriate buttons are pressed when the correct operation has been identified. This may introduce a different objective in the teaching of arithmetic and may present further explorations where word problems are involved.

WORD PROBLEMS IN ARITHMETIC

The use of a calculator presupposes that a problem can be interpreted into symbolic form appropriate to input into a calculator. This is not always a simple task and word problems will present pupils with numerous difficulties. As well as presenting learners with a reading task, verbal (word) problems will present both linguistic and interpretative difficulties. If their goal is to provide a link between mathematics and real life then they go about it in a clumsy way and in fact interpose between the two things they are intended to link. Deciding what the mathematical problem actually is, is a difficulty which never arises in a genuine problem situation. Furthermore, teachers should reconsider what pupils learn from problems that no one needs to solve, from stories which do not tell anything (they ask) and from tasks which seem designed to conceal rather than reveal what one is supposed to do. Consider the following word problem used in the CSMS (Concepts in Secondary Mathematics and Science) Project reported in Hart (1981):

> A shop makes sandwiches. You can choose from 3 sorts of bread and 6 sorts of filling. How do you work out how many different sandwiches you can choose?

When asked to circle the correct calculation '6 × 3' from among eight possible symbolic expressions there was a 43 per cent success rate among a sample of 81 twelve-year-olds' tested in mainstream schools across the country. Clearly few pupils, if any, in the lower ability bands were able to tackle this task.

In order to identify a solution procedure and then solve the problem, the following questions arise:

(i) Does the pupil possess the necessary reading skills to read the words?

(ii) Can the pupil interpret the meaning and identify the problem to be solved?

(iii) Does the pupil know an appropriate mathematical procedure for solving the problem?

(iv) Does the pupil have the relevant mathematical knowledge to solve the problem?

Perhaps the most pertinent question of all is whether they would consider this an appropriate question to ask since the real life situation would undoubtedly involve a practical rather than arithmetic solution.

It may well be that when the problem has been identified as a multiplication, a strategy involving multiplication or addition facts will be needed and yet is not available. Inability to find the correct solution to such problems may arise from lack of a procedure to identify that $6 \times 3 = 18$.

Research has shown that the difficulties associated with reading can also signal other aspects of mathematical learning that may cause problems. Pupils with reading difficulties would appear to have fewer number facts available for immediate use (Ackerman *et al.*, 1986). In recall of multiplication facts it has been claimed (Miles, 1983; Pritchard *et al.*, 1989) that a cohort of pupils described as 'dyslexics' have fewer number facts available than the control groups. Not surprisingly, poor memory and weakness at mathematics are associated (Webster, 1979) and this will particularly affect arithmetic where facility with numbers relies on the interconnection of processes and results about numbers.

In their discussion of reading skills, Shuard and Rothery (1984) explore the whole process by which a pupil uses the written words and any pictorial material to obtain its meaning. They consider the readability of mathematics texts and discuss characteristics of mathematical writing that are known to cause problems for the learner. But help with reading will not overcome all the problems as mathematics typically uses a vocabulary and syntax that reflects the formality associated with rigour and objectivity, and this results in texts that are less than user friendly. The visual appearance of texts is commented upon by Shuard and Rothery who note that the layout may lead to confusion or is regularly ignored by the learner rather than being used to help interpret meanings from the images. Further discussion of these aspects of language will be considered in Chapter 6.

INTERPRETING SYMBOLS IN ARITHMETIC

The problem of interpreting arithmetic symbols presents formidable obstacles for some. These may range from the meanings of the symbols '+, −, ×, ÷' to such symbols as '=' and the decimal point '.'. Take for example the multiplication symbol. When teachers were asked to say how the expression '3 × 4' should be read (Anghileri, 1985), various responses including '3 times 4', '3 multiplied by 4', '3 lots of 4', '3 fours' and '4 threes' suggested a lack of consensus about the meaning of the symbols. Does 3 × 4 relate to a set of 3 taken 4 times or to a set of 4 taken 3 times?

Both interpretations may be correct but each relates to a different verbal expression and different visual imagery. It may not at first appear to be a significant problem for both result in the same product, '12' , but many pupils' difficulties arise from ambiguous interpretations of symbolic forms particularly where they model the situation with apparatus or try to visualize an image to match the symbols.

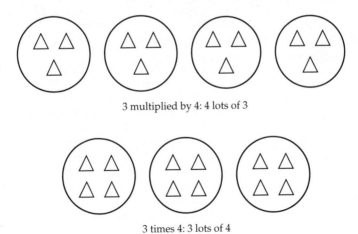

3 multiplied by 4: 4 lots of 3

3 times 4: 3 lots of 4

Figure 5.1 *Two interpretations of 3 × 4*

Division is another example where discrepancies in the interpretation of the symbol may go unnoticed by the teacher but inhibit learners in their progress towards a solution. The symbolic expression $12 \div 3$ may correctly be interpreted by pupils as '12 divided into 3' or as '12 divided into 3s' although the phrase 'divided by 3' is conventionally correct. (The pupils' words may be associated with dividing things in a real-life situation. Dividing a cake or pizza *'into 3'* may well lie within the experience of many pupils).

Both phrases suggest a procedure for solving the problem beyond the more formal interpretation '12 divided by 3'. But each interpretation indicates a different solution procedure, the first relates to a sharing of 12 into 3 equal sets, the second relates to groupings of 3.

Jody and Anna used a standard interpretation of the symbolic expression $6000 \div 6 =$ as 'How many sixes in six thousand?' They struggled to find a solution to the problem using the base ten apparatus of small cubes, rods, flats and large cubes representing 1, 10, 100 and 1000. Having assembled six piles each containing 1000 cubes or the equivalent in flats and rods they were keen to find out how many sixes could be removed. The teacher attempted to intervene to discuss alternative strategies but the girls were unable to identify any alternative interpretations to the problem.

These problems with the interpretation of symbols frequently cause confusion and low-attaining pupils rarely have a repertoire of procedures necessary to tackle all the types of problem that may arise. Teachers' interpretation of symbols may not be consistent. Sometimes a mathematics teacher and a support teacher working with the same pupil will offer different phrases and often different procedures for the solution of problems. Consistency within the classroom is important but may not overcome confusion that has arisen when teachers, parents, relatives and friends have all been involved at various stages helping with the solution of arithmetic problems. It is important to discuss with individual pupils their personal interpretations and understandings of the symbols involved. Peer group discussion and negotiation of meanings provides a valuable opportunity for teachers to observe and analyse the different understandings that may be evident within a class. Observation of pupils' efforts to solve problems will also reveal strategies that may be naive and inefficient even where effective.

NAIVE STRATEGIES

With difficulties of recall for both number facts and standard algorithms, many pupils will continue to use naive strategies, including finger methods, for calculations that may appear to be very simple. There are complexities that are not always appreciated by the busy teacher and close observations will enable the teacher to establish where understanding is evident and work from naive strategies towards an understanding of some of the relationships that are fundamental to arithmetic. Sometimes there is substantial under-standing evident in what may appear to the teacher (and to the pupil) to be naive methods.

Consider, for example, the complexities that may arise from simple calculations like

$$17 - 2 = \quad \text{and} \quad 17 - 15 =$$

Using fingers to count back in the first example will lead to two fingers being raised accompanied by the utterances '16, 15' the final utterance giving the answer 15. The second calculation, $17 - 15 =$ may also be accomplished by counting backwards to 15, again extending two fingers one at a time accompanied by the utterances '16, 15'. This time the answer is the number of fingers that are held up, i.e. 2. Many adults will also use fingers to support apparently simple calculations e.g. how many days between Friday and the following Tuesday. Teachers do not always appreciate the skills young people incorporate into finger methods and the implicit understanding they may be exhibiting. Time is needed to observe the pupils doing calculations and then help them advance in their understanding.

Finger methods for multiplication and division are even more com-plex than addition and as demonstrated by the following example:

Lisa (12.2) was attempting to calculate how many beads would be needed to make a necklace using six different colours with three beads of each colour. She began by extending three fingers on her right hand saying '1, 2, 3' and tallying this with one finger on her left hand. Then she said '4, 5, 6' as she counted the same three fingers of her right hand with the appropriate second tally finger extended on her left hand. When, at the next stage, she arrived at three fingers extended on each hand she became totally confused and looked from hand to hand and abandoned the count.

Now she started a second count, extending in turn all her fingers and counting rhythmically, '1, 2, 3 ... 4, 5, 6 ... 7, 8,

9 ... 10, 11, 12 ... 13, 14, 15 ... 16, 17, 18 ... 19, 20, 21 ... 22, 23, 24 ...' but she had not kept a tally of the threes counted and would have continued if she had not been interrupted and reminded of the task.

Being persistent, and confident she could find the total required, she now achieved a correct answer by using all her fingers, working from right to left and grouping them in threes, '1, 2, 3 ... that's one three. 1, 2, 3 ... that's two threes. 1, 2, 3 ... that's three threes. 1 (now returning to the beginning finger) 2, 3 ... that's four threes. 1, 2, 3 ... that's five threes. 1, 2, 3 ... that's six threes'.

She now counted all the fingers she had raised, remembering where she had to stop.

She had good understanding of the task and enough different finger strategies to succeed.

Here was a substantial achievement that prepared the way for a fruitful discussion about the roles of the two numbers in multiplication, one indicating the groupings and the other tallying how many groups. Later this was extended to explore commutativity and to consider why 6 threes give the same total as 3 sixes.

What Lisa had not achieved was any form of abstraction beyond using her fingers to represent the beads of a necklace. Her methods will enable solution of simple tasks set in real contexts but may not be transferable to those problems set in a symbolic or more formalized context.

The problem with naive strategies, even where they are effective in finding solutions, is that pupils are frequently inhibited from progress to more complex problems.

Lisa, for example was highly amused at the problem $4 \div \frac{1}{2}$. She read this as 'four shared by half' reflecting the sharing strategy she always used for division. She then went into hoots of laughter with her friends over the image of half a person sharing four sweets! In order to progress, pupils must appreciate that different interpretations are appropriate sometimes and must develop a variety of strategies for tackling each task. They must develop an appreciation of the links between arithmetic operations and establish connections between words and symbols.

MAKING CONNECTIONS

One of the major issues in the learning of mathematics is that of relating language and written symbols to both practical experience and particular procedures. Hughes (1986) has provided strong evidence of the benefits, if not necessity, of making explicit connections between the formal world of school mathematics and the intuitive mathematical worlds inhabited by young children. Haylock (1982) also makes a plea for more attention to teaching older pupils to make connections between forms of mathematical experience and expression. Jones and Haylock (1985) went further and proposed a practical activity for classroom use which is designed to help make links between the auditory inputs of mathematical language, specific activities and mathematical symbols and pictures. Using the slogan 'understanding means making connections' they introduced the 'Think Board' as a way of avoiding the inert, sterile, rote learning that they argue results from new learning when it remains in isolation from previous learning. On the basis of Haylock's (1982) suggestion there are four ways in which pupils may experience mathematics: mathematical language, symbols, concrete experience (actual or imagined) and pictures. Jones and Haylock argue that the teacher should work towards encouraging and rewarding the making of connections. They present the Think Board (see Figure 5.2) as a game-like activity for classroom use. This Think Board usually appears as a teacher-made device about the size of a conventional game board providing familiar objects for use by the pupils in the process of moving around the four sides.

The four elements of the game board are usually: numerals and signs (mathematical symbols of the experiences of handling number); pictures (pictorial representations of number e.g. number lines); real things (counters and blocks etc.) and stories (imagined concrete experiences embodied in word problems). The 'game' is for pupils to move from one element of the board to another swapping one form of representation for another. The teacher provides a starting point and returns to discuss the pupils' explanations and justifications for the transformations that they have used. Jones and Haylock (1985) observed that pupils used mathematical language as a medium for developing understanding. In the process of playing the game they gradually clarified and refined their use of mathematical phrases. They also note the beneficial affective consequences of this type of mathematical activity:

> In particular, groups of mathematically low attaining children have seemed to benefit considerably from the activity. Most mathematical tasks they are given to do are closed, requiring the provision of one correct answer. Too often their experience in such tasks is, failure. But here the task is much more open ended, with many acceptable responses. They seemed to tackle the activity with much less anxiety than they normally show in mathematics and clearly regarded it as non threatening. Their confidence, involvement, commitment and willingness to talk about mathematics all contrasted with their normal behaviour in mathematics lessons. (p. 34)

Removable card or plastic numerals
and signs (or words)

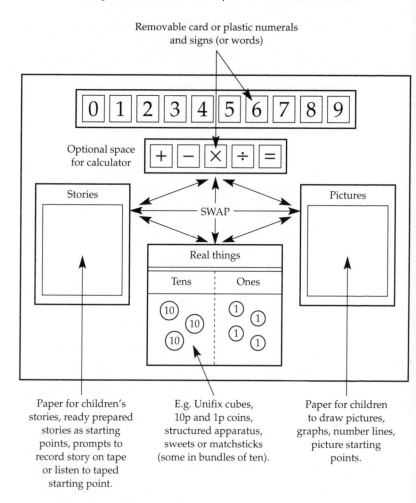

Figure 5.2 *The Think Board*
Source: Jones and Haylock (1982), p. 32.

This finding supports the position adopted by Parmar and Cawley (1991) on the extent to which the tasks set to pupils who experience difficulty in learning renders them passive. Larcombe (1985) adopts the term 'affective filter' to describe the impact of emotional matters on the perception of mathematics in schools. The Think Board (see Figure 5.2) may provide one way of helping pupils to readjust their 'filters' and break out of the cycles of anxiety, fear and panic (see Buxton, 1981) and passivity. It represents one approach to connecting up the different forms of mathematical understanding that may become isolated in particular forms of language use.

The difficulty for the classroom teacher remains that of maintaining a dialogue between that which is 'schooled' and that which is 'everyday'. Classroom processes which serve to connect the respective language domains and maintain instructional direction are not well developed. They either tend to celebrate the particular, local meanings held by the pupil at the expense of enabling access to mathematical generality or seek to reduce mathematics to such an extent that classrooms become places where learners are rendered passive and knowledge remains inert and isolated from the real world. The way forward would appear to be in the guise of the kind of pedagogy discussed in Chapter 3 along with some of the specific modifications discussed here.

ERRORS

When opportunities are made for observing pupils involved in mathematical thinking, there is substantial evidence (Hart, 1981) that pupils consistently use wrong or inappropriate strategies. As a sequel to the CSMS project already referred to, the Strategies and Errors in Secondary Mathematics (SESM) Project (1980–83) investigated in depth some of the difficulties experienced and strategies commonly used by secondary school pupils. The project found that observation and analysis of errors provides a powerful means for analysing pupil understanding (Booth, 1984) and that diagnostic assessment can become a valuable prerequisite for appropriate interactions. Newman (1977) uses a classification of errors based on analysis of the responses of twelve-year-olds to written tasks that may provide the framework for diagnostic approaches to be used by teachers. Clements (1980) uses this classification in his study of low achievers and his results suggest that reading and comprehension difficulties may play a crucial role in pupils low attainment in mathematics. Clements points out that even deeper probing is necessary to clarify more precisely the nature of difficulties within each category. There would still appear to be much to be done in this direction. HMCI (OFSTED, 1993b) reports 'time spent on number in some schools was excessive and ineffective: insufficient attention was given to sorting out whether errors were careless or represented misconceptions that needed particular attention'.

Young people who have difficulty with mathematics often use systematic routines that yield wrong answers. If it is conceptual misunderstandings that lie at the heart of many error-generating procedures then these misunderstandings are what should be addressed in instruction. In a study of efforts to make sense of new mathematics instruction, Resnick *et al.* (1989) suggest that different curriculum sequences influence the probability that certain types of error will occur. They also argue that it is inherent in the nature of teaching and learning that error generating rules will be acquired and that above all they provide valuable sources of information about understanding when used as diagnostic tools.

Wood proposes that interview techniques should be regarded as an essential aspect of teaching. In a re-reading of the CSMS interviews as teaching he provides an example of how discussion of the processes of thinking in problem solving can serve to help pupils discover how to achieve success where they had originally failed. In the following example of a pupil trying to subtract 28 from 51 the interviewer reminds the young person of a step that she has 'overlooked':

Maria	Do you take the top from the bottom? (Tries and takes one from eight, writing seven in the answer). Can't take five from two – have to take one of these (indicates 1 in 51).
Interviewer	Explain what you did there.
M	Crossed out the one (of 51) and put nought (in its place) and put the one on there (i.e. to the left of five to make it 15).
I	What was that to do? Why did you do that?
M	I put one on the tens.
I	OK. Right, now what are you going to do?
M	That's wrong.
I	Why is it wrong?
M	I'm supposed to take 15 from two and not two from fifteen.
I	Can we do it the other way? Can we do it this time so that we take the bottom from the top one?
M	Is that how we are supposed to do it?
I	That's how you usually do it, yes.

(from Wood, 1988)

This is a clear example of the way in which the focus of the teacher's attention can become the learner's own thought process. Once aware of the way in which the problem is being solved appropriate and meaningful advice can be given. Teachers may then begin to build on the basis of understanding possessed by the child rather than trying to superimpose a new order of understanding that may serve to create and or compound confusion.

The examples given below are drawn from Daniels (1993b) and provide an illustration of the complexity of 'answers' which are generated from procedures with relatively simple errors in the procedures themselves rather than their execution. In Example A a pupil who instead of 'carrying a number' writes the figure in the 'answer'. Hence in A:

$4 + 6 = 10$ (write down 10); $7 + 5 = 12$ (write down 12). The 'answer' is '1210'.

Example A

74	35	67	56
+56	+92	+18	+97
1210	127	715	1413

In Example B subtraction is carried out irrespective of the relative positions of the numbers. Thus in $245 - 137$; '5 from 7 gives 2; 3 from 4 gives 1; 1 from 2 gives 1; The answer is 112'.

Example B

32	245	524	135
−16	−137	−298	−67
24	112	374	132

In Example C multiplication is confused by the strategy of adding the number to be carried to the next figure in the multiplicand. Hence in C (b) (27×4) the child uses a procedure that follows the steps: $4 \times 7 = 28$; write down 8 , carry the 2 and add it to the 2 of 27 giving 4; now $4 \times 4 = 16$; write down 16; the answer is 168.

Example C

a	b	c	d
	2	2	1
34	27	18	24
×2	×4	×3	×4
68	168	94	126

In order to teach these young people there are certain requirements of a classroom situation, there must be a willingness to consider what the learner is doing as well as the outcome of calculations. It is usually better to abandon conventional algorithms and start at the point where the pupils' thinking has taken them. This takes time. Pupils' strategies are often complex and difficult to understand and misunderstandings are sometimes deliberately obscured in the hope that survival will extend to the end of another lesson. A few minutes 'explanation' is unlikely to wipe away an understanding that a pupil has developed over many years even where this understanding is obviously erroneous to the teacher.

Above all there is a need for the teacher to engage with what may be best described as the unofficial mathematical culture of the young person in order to understand the, often faulty, procedures. Building up from a starting point the pupil does understand, the teacher may help to make a connection with the often more powerful official procedures of the classroom (Daniels, 1993b).

This will be essential if pupils are to progress to more complex (and more interesting) problems. As well as the need to review their own procedures in order to eliminate efforts, the practice of reflecting on and discussing their own and other pupils methods will help develop the concepts and language of generalizations in mathematics. To be able to observe and comment upon procedures will help to lay the foundations for abstractions and for other areas of mathematics such as algebra.

ABSTRACTING

The move to abstraction and symbolization is probably the most crucial for developing confidence in pupils who experience difficulty with mathematics. By level 4 of the National Curriculum, pupils are expected to 'make general statements about patterns' and 'use simple formulae expressed in words'. The very words 'equations' and 'formulae' are daunting for many able adults whose experiences with algebra do not conjure up favourable memories. Among these adults are many parents and support teachers closely involved with pupils with Special Needs. But the ideas of pattern that underlies much in the National Curriculum Attainment Target on Algebra have appeal to adults and pupils and patterns may be found in many different areas of mathematics and in everyday life. An example, 'Growing Triangles' based on the practical activity of colouring in triangles of various sizes on isometric (triangular grid) paper shows how patterns may be the starting point for generalizing and abstracting.

Several triangles with different length sides can be coloured or cut out before trying to link the number of little triangles with the length of the sides. Groups of pupils can pool their findings and try to present them in some systematic way. Counting little triangles in those with sides of length five or more can be tedious and it becomes effective to note that a triangle of side four with another row of triangles added to the bottom gives a triangle of side five. Cutting up some of the triangles into strips will verify this and it may be expressed in the pupils words as a generalization.

Expressing this relationship in symbols will lead to the pattern of numbers:

1
1 + 3
1 + 3 + 5
1 + 3 + 5 + 7

involving *odd* numbers and totals that are the *square* numbers: 1, 4, 9, 16 ... Strange to find the square numbers relating to triangles! Using a calculator to find the squares of larger numbers will provide an efficient means of determining the results for larger and larger triangles, some of which may be verified by further experimentation on the isometric paper.

Linking this with the areas of different sized squares may be the start of investigations on squared paper, to find how the same number patterns will be replicated for squares.

Linking square and square numbers may help justify the naming of such numbers and give pupils visual images to connect with the more abstract number pattern.

Describing and generalizing relationships, particularly those involving number patterns, forms the basis for the National Curriculum in Algebra. Popular conceptions of algebra in secondary school involves the use of letters in equations and formulae and the expression of abstract relationships with mathematical symbols. The ability to observe and express relationships may develop with experience when pupils talk about their work and discuss their observations. Collaborative work with other pupils may provide a setting in which they begin to develop the basis of formulating equations. There is a need to work from a position of understanding e.g. 'area means counting squares' to algebraic expressions like 'area is the number in each row times the number of rows' which provides a more meaningful statement than 'area = length × width'.

Costello (1991) summarizes a section on algebra for eleven to sixteen year olds in the National Curriculum by suggesting three main principles which might lead to effective teaching and learning of algebra:

Firstly, the potentially most profitable basis for a study of algebra is probably not found in 'missing number' problems, which turn into equations to be solved. Rather, algebra is rooted in the awareness of number patterns, relationships and generalisations.

Secondly, the introduction of a new approach or technique needs to be presented in a justifying and motivating context. Often this context will be familiar and 'real'; but it need not be, providing a problem can be identified which cannot readily be solved with existing skills. What is somewhat fruitless is the development of sophisticated machinery to solve problems which can be solved adequately without such paraphernalia.

Thirdly, the range of available approaches should be recognised, and sensible choices made. (p. 40)

For pupils with Special Needs there must be an emphasis on describing and generalizing findings that relate to real experiences. For many such pupils, there will be a heavy reliance on teacher interaction to encourage verbalization of observations that the pupils cannot write or symbolize. Further consideration of particular aspects of algebra are beyond the scope of this book but the teaching experiments described in Booth (1984) and the findings of the CSMS project will provide a rich source of further reading in this area.

TEACHER INTERACTIONS

Classrooms where pupils are using unconventional approaches to problem solving may well also be places where the teachers find the mathematical behaviour of their pupils beyond their experience. The confusion is often compounded by the reluctance of the young people to reveal their own strategies because they have learned, through the way in which their mathematical failure has been treated in the past, NOT to reveal too much about the way they think and learn for fear of ridicule. This is compounded by assessment procedures relating to the National Curriculum, where the teacher may be charged with inflating performance, where possible, for reporting purposes, when the most effective assessment may be diagnostic in nature, aimed at revealing misunderstanding. What becomes clear when detailed considerations of content of the mathematics curriculum are undertaken is the need for sensitive understanding of the implications for the learner. Language and symbolization often provide the key to understanding. They may also present the pupil with learning difficulties and problems they are unable to overcome without substantial intervention from a teacher whose personal appreciation of the nature of mathematical relationships is not well developed.

Many of the teachers who end up teaching low-attaining pupils in secondary schools are themselves insecure about mathematics:

Mathematics . . . is in my experience particularly prone to ad hoc staffing for the 'bottom sets' in ordinary schools. It is not very difficult to find teachers who were not trained – and had never intended to teach the subject – involved in mathematics with the least able pupils . . . In certain cases I have seen very low ability pupils whose mathematics lessons are shared between as many as three different non-specialist teachers. The pupils draw their own conclusions about the status and worth of mathematics so do the staff.

(from Larcombe, 1985)

As HMCI (OFSTED, 1993b) notes this would still seem to be the case in many schools:

> In almost all the schools, however, some teaching of mathematics was carried out by teachers with no initial qualifications or relevant experience or recent in-service training (INSET) in mathematics. Usually these non-specialist staff did not teach more than one or two classes. Some of these non-specialists were insecure in subject knowledge and lacked awareness of the statutory order and assessment requirements. (p. 24)

Children often present teachers with confusing approaches to mathematical problems. The example given below is typical of the seemingly bizarre type of protocol that may be partially revealed in a mathematics classroom.

$194 - 89 = ?$ (The problem as presented to the child (age 9.8))

(Talk) You leave the one over the side.
1 (Action)
(Talk) Then with the 94 you got left you put 9 lines down and put the 4 to the next of the line.
1 ///////// 4 (Action)
(Talk) Then you get the 89 and you cross off 8 of the lines.
1 XXXXXXXX / 4 (Action)
(Talk) Then with the last line you cross that out and that's the 9 of the 89.
1 XXXXXXXXX 4 (Action)
(Talk) Then with the one that is left over you add it to the 4 and you have got your answer.

Such interactions can provide a positive opportunity to reconsider meanings and reflect on strategies if teachers have the time and confidence to share mathematical thinking. Pupils best attempts must be encouraged and not undermined if they are to invest the effort needed to re-negotiate meanings and methods. There is nothing more satisfying than reaching a successful conclusion to a demanding task in mathematics. Classroom approaches must seek to reward effort with success by providing tasks that have the appropriate balance of challenge and support for all the individuals who will be involved. This is itself the challenge for mathematics and support staff together.

Thus in order to act as a supporter and guide of pupil development a teacher must feel sufficiently confident to participate in discussions about mathematics in which the mathematical logic may be unfamiliar to him/her. The multitude of ways in which pupils come to understand the significance of mathematical signs and symbols and the meaning of word problems may influence the way they use and understand the use of devices like calculators. They may develop highly personalized approaches to number competence and use naive strategies in a variety of circumstances. They may seek to deliberately obscure the procedures they use from the gaze of their teachers. Thus any teacher attempting to 'decode' a pupil's mathematical understanding is faced with a complex and often very demanding problem to solve. In order to 'tune in to' their pupils they have to find ways of facilitating discussion, which may be construed as threatening.

Perhaps the most important leap for teachers, who may formerly have seen themselves as the transmitter of mathematical truths, is to accept that young learners develop their own ways of coping with mathematics. Their ways may well be different from 'ours'. The teaching task is to connect with and then help to develop that which the pupil brings to the classroom.

SUMMARY

We have focused in this chapter on a number of issues that we feel are particularly pertinent to learners with SEN whose strategies may not always conform to the ways that have been taught and who may experience particular difficulties. By watching and listening to pupils, teachers can come to understand better the process of learning mathematics in the classroom and we have considered examples that illustrate this point. The examples we use are drawn mainly from arithmetic as this exposes many difficulties relating to language and symbols that will remain fundamental to mathematics learning generally. In doing so we do not wish mathematics to be identified exclusively with number work but point to other chapters where wider considerations provide a more balanced view of the content of mathematics in a curriculum appropriate for all pupils.

It has been possible to provide only a 'snapshot' of some of the research results that are available to help teachers analyse their practice in relation to some of the evidence available on childrens' learning. For the interested teacher, further reading is available in an accessible form in Dickson *et al. Children Learning Mathematics: A Teacher's Guide to Recent Research* (1984).

─6─

Language and communication

This chapter is concerned with language and communication in the broadest sense. It examines boundaries and barriers in communicative practices. We start with a discussion of the cognitive significance of communication practices within the context of the current definitions of mathematics in schools. The next section is concerned with the relationship *between* the everyday mathematical world of the pupil and the mathematical world of schools. Here the boundaries that exist between school mathematics and the mathematics of everyday life will be explored and their pedagogic significance discussed. This is followed by a discussion of the practices of communication **within** the classroom. The issues in the use of speech and written language in the mathematics classroom will be explored in terms of barriers to communication and ways of alleviating difficulties.

THE IMPORTANCE OF LANGUAGE USE IN SUBJECTS

Just as different academic disciplines may be said to have their own 'languages' so different groupings or orderings of the content of a particular curriculum may be thought of as having their own 'dialects'. The particular form of mathematics that is taught in school will, by this analysis, have its own particular language demands. Thus the content of the mathematics curriculum may be significant in terms of the specific language demands it makes on pupils.

Much has been written to the effect that learning to talk the language of school subjects is the essence of learning the subject. Without access to the appropriate aspects of the language of mathematics pupils may be restricted in their use of strategies *for thinking* and for problem solving. Their restricted set of strategies may function well in specific circumstances yet may not draw benefit from the depth and breadth of formal mathematical culture. This culture may itself be seen as a set of social practices:

> When we say that the mastery of physics or literary criticism means being able to talk physics like a physicist or write analyses like a critic,

we are talking about making the meanings of physics and literary criticism using the resources of spoken and written language. Talking physics and writing criticism are social practices. They are parts of larger social activities. They are learned socially, function socially, and are socially meaningful. Spoken and written language are social resources for making social meaning.

(Lemke, 1988, p. 82)

Here then is a theoretical position which may be seen to support the development of means of access to what might be termed the 'official' mathematical discourse.

The Cockcroft Report argues that language plays an essential part in the formulation and expression of mathematical ideas. A quote from a headteacher is given in paragraph 306, 'there is a need for more talking time ... ideas and findings are passed on through language and developed through discussion, for it is this discussion after the activity that finally sees the point home'. It may be that 'seeing the point home' refers to the acquisition of an aspect of formal mathematical understanding and that the term 'ideas passed on through language' refers to the dialogues in which connections are made between one form of understanding and another.

The emphasis on oral work in the Cockcroft recommendation finds an echo in much of the social psychology that is subsumed in the constructivist tradition in mathematics education discussed in Chapter 3. Speech and written language are, by definition, the tools of mathematical dialogue. Without access to these tools pupils are constrained to use everyday language which may not facilitate the development of some aspects of mathematical thought. In the most recent translation of Chapter 6 of *Thinking and Speech* Vygotsky claims a particular function of speech in instruction within schooling:

The instruction of the child in systems of scientific knowledge in school involves a unique form of communication in which the word assumes a function which is quite different from that characteristic of other forms of communication ...

1. The child learns word meanings in certain forms of school instruction not as a means of communication but as part of a system of knowledge.
2. This learning occurs not through direct experience with things or phenomena but through other words.

(Rieber and Carton, 1987, p. 27)

By Vygotsky's argument, tools, whether practical or symbolic, are initially external i.e. used outwardly on nature or in communicating with others. But tools affect their users: language used first as a communicative tool finally shapes the minds of those who adapt to its use (Bruner, 1987).

Following this argument, if independent cognitive functioning is initially acquired in a social/communicative context then communication difficulty must bear with it consequences for the pattern of cognitive development. If children were to be denied access to one channel of communication, one form of psychological tool, then, according to Vygotsky, cognitive development may follow a qualitatively different pathway from that expected by teachers. Similarly different contexts may demand different kinds of mathematical activity and obtain different outcomes.

Wood *et al.* (1984) demonstrated that the difference in mathematical ability between hearing impaired and deaf children may not result from deafness *per se* but from a differing form of educational experience. It was argued that even quite mild hearing loss interferes with the child's social interaction and communication to such an extent that the social foundations of their early mathematical development is disrupted. The average deaf child leaves secondary school with a mathematical performance that may be expected of a twelve year old. At one level this may be seen as a surprising finding. If a deaf child is placed in a classroom in which a scheme of individualized worksheets is used to deliver the curriculum then oral communication difficulties should not impair mathematical performance. However, this statement ignores the complexity of the language and communication difficulties that may be associated with hearing impairment. Barham and Bishop (1991) show how the language of mathematics can cause specific difficulties for pupils with such problems. Clearly words which embody minor differences in terms of auditory discrimination but signify fundamental mathematical differences constitute a potential source of confusion, for example, 'sixty' and 'sixteen'. The general ambiguity in spatial terms in mathematics, the variety of terms used for one function, and particularly logical connectives (and, or, if . . . then) which are rarely directly taught, can all come to interfere with making progress in mathematics:

> When considering children's understanding of multiplication, individuals were asked to make 'pattern sticks' with linking cubes using 'five different colours and three cubes of each colour'. Several children presented a stick of 8 cubes consisting of five different colours together with three further cubes of one colour. Talking about the stick they had made revealed that their interpretation was 'five different colours and three cubes'. The vital word *each* had been ignored. Some children were unable to modify their sticks even when emphasis was placed on the word 'each' and they were given a second opportunity. In multiplication, understanding of the word 'each' is vital but it is not taught.
>
> (from Anghileri, 1991)

Everyday word meanings are usually assumed in the classroom but the above example illustrates how the significance of particular words can easily be overlooked by pupils where their interpretation is vital for mathematical meaning.

Barham (1988) suggests that microcomputers can help to provide a mode of communication which can help to make mathematics more accessible. The rationale for this recommendation is couched in terms of attention, motivation, potential for repetition, differentiation into levels of difficulty, and variety of means or tools for engagement with the machine. This list highlights the need to consider the broader consequences of a communication difficulty as well as the immediate language demands of a particular task. That communication difficulties may carry affective consequences in schools is on the one hand all too obvious but often ignored.

Another issue often associated with particular difficulties and/or disabilities is the assumption of uniformity in instructional needs within a particular group. Perhaps this should not be too surprising given the tendency in schools, as witnessed by HMI (1989c), (and given popular support by senior politicians) to consider class teaching as an appropriate strategy for meeting instructional needs. Children who experience language impairments constitute such a diverse group with such complex patterns of causation that suggestions beyond a fairly minimal set are often inappropriate for individuals. Donlan and Hutt (1991) offer such a set for children with language disorders:

> Direct teaching to ensure that the following take place:
> 1. Teaching the number system 1–100 and place value.
>   a. Use systematic visual patterns to aid learning.
>   b. Give separate consideration to the auditory/verbal component of any task, and structure its requirements to suit the needs of particular learners.
> 2. Teach counting.
> 3. Teach time concepts. (p. 205)

In essence their argument is that teachers should try and consider those aspects of mathematical development that are often assumed in mathematical tasks in secondary schools and identify those items which have not been acquired and thus require direct teaching. For the non-specialist SEN teacher, the SENCO and the classroom teacher, this initial strategy seems appropriate within Stage I of the Code of Practice. Pupils with marked communication difficulties in secondary schools should have been assessed at Stage 3 before leaving primary school and thus should come to benefit either directly or indirectly via their teacher from the advice and support from a suitably qualified specialist. The needs of these pupils are not within the scope of this book.

COMMON SENSE IN LANGUAGE

The problem for the educator may be cast in terms of moving from the everyday context of 'common sense' mathematics with its everyday language into the world of the mathematical culture of schools with its own language demands. Ultimately this is a move from the particular to the general; a move from local, often context bound, language and understanding to the more context independent language practices of school mathematics.

> To become truly proficient at mathematics one must be able, eventually, to reason with and on the formal symbols themselves. Part of the power of algebra, for example, is that once an appropriate set of questions is written to express the quantities and relationships in a situation, it is possible to work through extensive transformations on the questions without having to think about the reference situations for the intermediate expressions that are generated. In this sense the 'meaning' of algebra is one that is legal within the formal system, and the application of correct transformation rules insures that all expressions that are generated will be legal. But every algebraic expression can also be interpreted in terms of the situations (quantities, relationships, etc.) to which it refers, and every transformation rule can be justified in terms of the ways in which quantities behave under certain kinds of transformations. These references provide an alternative meaning for algebraic expressions and transformation rules.
>
> (Resnick, 1986, p. 37)

The language of mathematics in this sense may come to provide a set of social psychological tools which may assume qualitatively different relations with specific contexts, from everyday language. Harris and Evans (1991) draw on some work of C. Hoyles to provide a summary of the differences between informal mathematics and school mathematics which extends the analysis beyond that of language to the more general nature of the different practices:

Informal mathematics	School mathematics
embedded in task	decontextualized
motivation is functional	motivation is intrinsic
objects of activity are concrete	objects of activity are abstract
	processes are named and are the object of study
data is ill defined and 'noisy'	data is well defined and presented tidily
tasks are particularistic	tasks are aimed at generalisation
accuracy is defined by the situation	accuracy is assumed or given
numbers are messy	numbers are arranged to work out well

Informal mathematics	School mathematics
work is collaborative, social correctness is negotiable language is imprecise and responsive to setting	work is individualistic answers are right or wrong language is precise and carefully differentiated (p. 129)

In achieving rigour and formalization in mathematics, language is 'selected' to reflect such formalization. The outcome is a language of formal communication that is alien to the everyday experiences of many children and adults. A useful example is found where the operation of multiplication is used and one number is '*multiplied by*' another. This passive construction may be contrasted to the active construction 'times' that is more generally used by non-mathematicians (Anghileri, 1991). Children use active constructions (Sam hit Tom) in preference to passive constructions (Tom was hit by Sam) and passive constructions are reserved for formal communications. Further discussion can be found in Beilin (1975) who suggests that *active* sentence forms are easier than *passive* forms 'in both their comprehension and their production'.

One of the major tasks for teachers in mathematics is that of helping to recognize the specific demands of the mathematics that pupils are faced with in school. What is clear is that the *real* demands of classrooms make the transition between the 'informal' and the 'schooled' difficult. Irrespective of the way in which it is constructed, the given mathematical content of the curriculum defines the criteria against which all pupils are judged and as such constitutes that which is powerful. This position on power and knowledge then requires an answer to questions about how to enable all pupils to have access to the official 'currency' of mathematics.

The following sections will consider issues of access in the communicative practices that exist within schools and of the relation between the mathematics of schooling and that of everyday life.

INFORMAL AND FORMAL

It is fruitful to consider ways in which children who experience difficulty in learning may be helped to engage with what Vygotsky terms 'the system of knowledge' as it exists in school mathematics. Consideration is necessary of approaches to the design and development of written materials and to the implications in terms of speech practices in attempts to enable pupils to have access to the language of mathematical meaning in school. The term 'mathematical meaning in school' is used deliberately as reference is being made to the mathematical knowledge which **counts** in schools today. There would seem to be two related processes of reform in school mathematics.

One of which is with respect to the content of the mathematics curriculum, the other is the kind of pedagogic reform discussed more generally in Chapter 3.

Noss (1991) provides an analysis which argues that the mathematical content of the curriculum may be seen to be culturally positioned and partial:

> Many, if not most of the children in western classrooms are confronted with the mathematics of which they are not, and perhaps have no wish to be, members. (p. 77)

Whilst this may be seen by some as a somewhat strong version of a particular way of viewing the situation it serves to raise the issue of the relationship between the mathematics of school and that of the 'outside' world.

Under the three headings of 'utilitarianism', 'mathematical anthropology' and 'cognition in practice', Dowling (1991) discusses developments in the arguments concerning the content of the mathematics curriculum. Specifically he examines the relationship between conent and context. Under the heading 'utilitarianism' he analyses the way in which much of the research sponsored in the wake of the Cockcroft Report sought to identify elements of an approach to mathematics in school which would provide pupils with a mathematical 'toolbox' for use in work and adult life. He argues that this work ironically provided a substantial body of evidence that there is a strong boundary between school mathematics and everyday life and suggests that the notion of the 'toolbox' is invalid. This point is illustrated through reference to a situation in which an attempt was made to bring maths into school from the everyday world of pupils.

> The pupils, at sixteen years of age, had failed consistently to master anything but the most elementary aspects of school mathematics. Every year they appear in the bottom 20 per cent at examination time . . . they had not developed the capacity for abstract thought. They had received and remained unhelped by considerable 'remedial' teaching and finally, they left school 'hating everyfink what goes on in maffs'. Yet in their spare time some of these people kept and raced pigeons. They understood the intricacies of the racing rules as part of the folklore of pigeon keeping; what the expert mathematician would recognise as 'mathematical knowledge' featured in, though remained undifferentiated from the rest of this knowledge.
>
> (Spradberry, quoted in Dowling, 1991, p. 102)

This author tried to draw on real life contexts in the teaching of mathematics in school, however his pupils rejected what he saw as 'relevant' and they saw as not being 'real maths'. Dowling also suggests that there are difficulties with the ways in which Mathematical Anthropology seeks to bring cultural diversity into school mathematics. He cautions that this movement still represents the 'colonisation' of diverse mathematical practices within schooling. This is a matter which has received considerable attention in discussions of matters of equality of opportunity in mathematics (e.g. Shan and Bailey, 1991).

The work discussed by Dowling under the 'cognition in practice' label develops an account of mathematical activity which is highly context specific (Lave, 1988). The social structuring of the context is related to the form of what may be taken as mathematics.

> School mathematics itself constitutes an activity, with its own goals and means, and with a distinctive rationality which cannot simply be transplanted into another activity – such as shopping.
>
> (Dowling, 1991, p. 110)

Dowling cautions against the tactic of attempting to transpose the mathematics of schooling onto everyday situations in a simplistic way. Presentation of artifical problems will inevitably lead pupils to question the 'point' of an exercise. Nunes *et al.* (1993) echo this concern when they present an overview of three different perspectives of schooling and cognitive development. In the first account, which draws heavily on the work of Vygotsky, they discuss two types of learning experience: 'bottom up' which gives rise to spontaneous concepts, and 'top down' which gives rise to scientific concepts. Spontaneous attempts to understand aspects of social and physical reality which provide local solutions to particular problems are contrasted with interactions in school when pupils are presented with concepts of general applicability.

The second account, the sociocognitive approach, is one in which schools create social situations that put children's concepts into conflict with others. In the third account, Nunes *et al.* bring these two accounts together as well as drawing on the work of Lave (1988) who argues that learning in school and out of school is connected to specific problem-solving practices. They suggest that:

1. The distinction between school arithmetic and street arithmetic is that between *written and oral* practices.
2. Mathematics problem solving in school is written and relies on procedures that distance it from meaning. This distance from meaning is an advantage in the sense that the forms used in schools are more general.
3. Oral practices preserve meaning.
4. . . . the differences between oral and written practices are not differences in how abstract the procedures are. Both procedures are of a general and abstract nature. The differences seem to stem from the amount of knowledge required of the subject about the specific

situation being handled. There seems to be a trade-off in oral and written arithmetic as far as preservation of meaning and generalizability are concerned.

(from Nunes *et al.*, 1993)

They advocate the principle of bringing street mathematics into the classroom and through this 'preserving meaning during the mathematizing of situations'. They follow Dowling in their warning against the presentation of artifical problems and advance the case for what they call 'realistic mathematics education' which involves:

1. Posing to pupils in the classroom problems that require the consideration of empirical constraints as well as social and logical rules that apply outside school.
2. Solving a problem involves making decisions about how to proceed in imagined situations.
3. (Recognising the) difficulty of thinking of good problems to work from in the classroom.
4. (The understanding that) problems that have easy mathematical solutions are in fact jokes, because the constraints of life are ignored in the problem-solving process. For example: There were ten birds in a tree; two were killed by a gunshot; how many were left? The arithmetic answer '8' violates assumptions about the outside world – all living birds would have flown away.

(from Nunes *et al.*, 1993)

Nunes *et al.* contrast real with unreal problems using the following examples:

1. A problem from realistic mathematics education.
   Tonight 81 parents will visit our school.
   At each table 6 parents can be seated.
   How many tables do we need?

2. An unrealistic problem about time.
   John ate 8 Big Macs. It takes John 15 minutes to eat a Big Mac.
   How long did it take him to eat them all?

Acknowledging the need for realistic mathematics problems, teaching will be most successful when pupils are themselves involved in the selection of tasks to stimulate their interest and to find solutions that are of personal significance. As noted in Chapter 2, such problems need not all be context bound since patterns and puzzles have wide appeal, can stimulate meaningful observations, generalizations and discussion and may incorporate much valuable mathematics.

Pupils' informal knowlege in mathematics

The other aspect of the relationship of between the 'schooled' and the everyday is concerned with the informal knowledge that pupils bring into school with them. Baroody (1984) suggests that children enter school with different levels of competencies and differences in their informal knowledge. It may be that pupils who experience difficulty in learning mathematics in school have not benefited from everyday (non-school) experiences which they are able to connect with their mathematical experiences in school. These children would find it more difficult to benefit from the 'informal knowledge that serves as a kind of cognitive underpinning or scaffolding for school learning', (Ginsburg and Allardice, 1984, p. 196).

Hiebert (1984) found that pupils tend to handle school mathematics via reference to their own informal mathematics. They *adapt* themselves to school mathematics rather than *adopt* its rules and procedures. School learning has been shown to improve when the informal strengths of everyday mathematics are exploited with pupils whose attainments are low (Russell and Ginsburg, 1984). If all children enter school with a wealth of informal knowledge, perhaps not the same informal knowledge, then schooling should attempt to capitalize and build upon this resource. Even though it may well be that the 'gap' between the everyday and the schooled is considerable for some pupils. Chapter 4 discussed the 'Think Board' propounded by Jones and Haylock. This kind of activity in which the role of the teacher is that of building on pupils' thinking to bridge the gap between informal knowledge and the more formal knowledge taught in school would seem to be of particular importance for many of the pupils whose attainments in mathematics are low. It would seem to be important for all pupils, including high-achieving pupils who are more able to cope with and manage the 'gap'. As outlined in Chapters 3 and 4, the effective teacher of children with SEN is likely to be one who probes and makes suggestions based on pupils' observations. The teacher would use the pupils' oral responses to questions and written work as guides and hints to pupil understanding and thus indicators of the kind of tasks and instruction that are really going to help. Trying to impose a pre-given method or procedure which does not take account of prior understanding and does not attempt to make connection is unlikely to be effective.

Spoken and written language in school

It has long been recognized that the use of written and spoken language in mathematics brings with it its own special concerns. Bangs (1993) notes that the majority of teachers in an NUT survey of the

National Curriculum in mathematics (as it was at that time) reported that the language demands, physical co-ordination and writing demands of mathematics SATs and particularly of number, handling data, organizing information, and probabilities, caused many difficulties. Bartlett and Peacey (1992) found support for this particularly with respect to readability at Key Stage 3.

Teachers have been exhorted to take care to monitor specific language issues in the mathematics classroom:

> They should take account of:
> Variation in the level of language skills of students;
> The variety of terms used for a particular mathematical expression;
> Some stylised expressions which may make it difficult for students to comprehend the problem and, therefore choose the correct solution.
> (Cockcroft Report, DES, 1982, para. 246)

Suggestions have been made for questions that teachers should ask when teaching pupils from a different cultural background from their own:

> Do the teacher and learner share the same (first) language?
> Do the teacher and learner share the same culture?
> Do the teacher and learner share the same logic and reasoning system?
> Is there a match between the language, culture and logic/reasoning system of pupil and teacher?
> (Strevens quoted in Shan and Bailey, 1991, p. 26)

The issue of bilingualism in special needs practices has received rather less attention than it deserves. This is, perhaps, particularly the case in mathematics. A recent paper by Clarkson and Galbraith (1992) provides a useful exposition of some of the main theoretical issues and highlights the inadequacy of much of the research data available in this area.

They draw on the work of Cummins (1979, 1984) who developed two hypotheses; the threshold hypothesis and the developmental interdependence hypothesis. Cummins initially distinguishes between people who learn a second language as a replacement for their mother tongue (a 'subtractive environment') and people who supplement their mother tongue through learning a second language (an 'additive environment'). He describes those who show similar competency in both languages as 'balanced bilinguals' and suggests that they are at a cognitive advantage over monolinguals when in an additive environment providing that they have passed some upper threshold in the second language. A lower threshold is said to exist in a subtractive environment. 'If students are in a subtractive learning environment with their language replacing their original language, then these students are worse off than students who are clearly dominant in one of the languages' (Clarkson and Galbraith, 1992, p. 35). Cummins further suggests that the level of competence in 'one language is partially a function of the student's competence in the other language'. This developmental interdependence hypothesis would suggest, according to Clarkson and Galbraith (1992), that mathematical strategies would transfer relatively easily across languages. In their study they report some support for the threshold hypothesis. They acknowledge that their work does not offer convincing support for all aspects of Cummins' theory but is suggestive of the importance of the development of research in the area. They provide a concluding cautionary note to their paper which is of importance in the present discussion:

> Bilingualism should not be treated as a single, unidimensional entity in research studies, and hence care should be exercised if global statements are made concerning bilingual students. At least one important dimension that should be considered is the extent of competence of each language that students exhibit . . . when categorised along this dimension, different performances on cognitive tasks (at least mathematical ones) may be evidenced. (p. 42)

Thus simplistic formulations of the kind of mathematical instruction that 'bilinguals need' are as inappropriate as simplistic formulations of what all children with SEN are sometimes said to 'need'. There is much to be done here.

In general there remains a tension between the temptation to make the language demands of instruction and participation in mathematics classes easier and the need to preserve the inherent school-based mathematical meanings that can only be accessed through specialized use of language.

When faced with the problem:

'Jane is 1m 17cm tall and her brother Paul is 1m 54cm tall. What is the difference between their heights?'

Kemal (11.2) was confused. With pressure on time, the teacher came to help by advising 'Difference between means "take away"'. Kemal became more confused. The idea of 'taking away' one height from another is probably conceptually more difficult than making a comparison, perhaps with the support of images on squared paper. It is common to find 'difference between' problems in subtraction and it is common for subtraction to be interpreted as 'take away' but the procedures involved do not always match the visual imagery that may help a child find solutions to such problems.

Given that pupils often find the language of mathematics in school confused and confusing it is, perhaps, not surprising that there have been attempts to simplify it. On the one hand Larcombe proposed a process of simplification of written material:

1. Worksheets should use as few words as possible. The vocabulary should be within the pupils' understanding.
2. Do not put too many questions on a sheet. This allows pupils the satisfaction of finishing a piece of work fairly often.
3. Ensure the layout is clear and visually stimulating and that not too much information is crammed on a page.
4. Use pictures where possible. Make them interesting.
5. Use typing or printing whenever possible.

(from Larcombe, 1978)

This approach certainly may be seen to reduce the cognitive load from one perspective but increase it from another. Following the lead of writers such as Frank Smith (1971), a reduction in the 'richness of contextual cueing' in the instructional text would make the task more demanding. Pupils confronted with a decontextualized, and often abstract text, are faced with the task of making sense of the information in the absence of contextual clues. 'Simple' tasks are often more difficult than 'complex' ones. The Cockcroft Report (DES, 1982) leads the way out of the dilemma with the suggestion that written instructional texts should only form part of an instructional regime proposing that means should be found for engaging pupils in the language of mathematics:

> The policy of trying to avoid reading difficulties by preparing work cards in which the use of language is minimised or avoided altogether should not be adopted. Instead the necessary language skills should be developed through discussion and explanation and by encouraging children to talk and write about the investigations they have undertaken. (para. 311)

If abstract tasks are to be presented they should be supported by conversation and the pupil should helped to make sense of them in collaboration with others.

The language demands of the 'schooled mathematics' constitute one of the major factors in the construction of difficulties in classroom contexts. These are demands that may be eased.

Ordinary English and Mathematical English

The issue of the relationship between the meaning of the word in mathematics education and its immediate context is discussed at length by Shuard and Rothery (1984). They suggest that this issue is complicated in the reading of mathematical texts because of the ways in which the meaning of the specialized technical vocabulary that exists in mathematics relates to the 'everyday' meaning associated with the same words. As they point out, there are some words which will have the same meaning in Mathematical English and what they refer to as Ordinary English, for example, 'because', 'cat', etc. Further there are some words which are only used within mathematical discourse, for example, 'parallelogram', 'coefficient' etc. However, there are also some words which have a different meaning in both. In some cases the meanings may have some connection ('gradient'), in others there may be no relation. Take for example the case of the word 'odd', a word which assumes very different meanings in different contexts. When the wrong meaning is used in a mathematical context confusion sets in.

Teacher: Is 5 an odd number?
Pupil: Yes – a bit – it's like 2 but different.
Teacher: You mean because 2 is an even number.
Pupil: No it's not even it's – 1 is even, 2 is lumpy like 5 but its lumps are different – that's why it's odd. 8 is even too.

Wood (1988) argues the case for negotiating the special and technical meanings of words with pupils as they engaged in mathematical activities. He emphasizes the importance of understanding the relations between everyday language and mathematical discourse. By way of illustration of the importance of this topic he offers the following example:

Interviewer: Do you know what volume means?
Child: Yes.
Interviewer: Could you explain to me what it means?
Child: Yes, it's what is on the knob of the television set. (p. 193)

However the APU (1989) reports that many pupils, particularly at secondary level do not consider that mathematics is something that is open to discussion and negotiation. They make a case for the simple procedure of asking pupils about their mathematical thinking as part of normal classroom practice. In a way that echoes much of the work on error analysis discussed in Chapter 4, they suggest that opening discussions with pupils is an important aspect of the process of teachers understanding pupil understanding. This is not necessary if the teacher conforms to the expectation of a formal transmission-based pedagogy in which the transfer of information is the focus of attention rather than the construction of understanding. Discussion and questioning may provide windows on to the construction process. The APU illustrate this with an extract from an interview with Jason who seemed to be capable of ordering one place decimals:

> Jason (reading the question out loud to the assessor): 'Put these decimals in order of size, smallest first: 0.064, 0.35, 0.64, 1.1. (says numbers 'Zero point zero six four, zero point three five, zero point six four, one point one').
>
> This looks a bit tricky at first . . . it looks a catch but its not really, I don't think, because 1.1 will go first because it's got a one at the start instead of a zero; so that will go highest 'cause I'm working my way down'.
>
> Then the second . . . this is a bit tricky the second one for me. I think they'd both share second, because it's got 0.64 and 0.064 and I don't think that the first zero after the point doesn't sort of matter . . . I think they'd share the same place . . . But there again that zero might mean zero a bit, sort of a bit down from the 0.64 . . . as an answer they'd be joint second and then as a last one it would be 0.35 'cause that is lower than 0.64 and 1.1'. (p. 20)

This transcript provides some insight into the thought processes of a pupil and makes it possible for the teacher to respond to the relevant instructional issues that could contribute to the pupil's understanding. Much of the APU study is concerned with the administration of tests. They also raise a number of important issues for teaching itself. The teachers and researchers who administered the assessment device found it hard not to 'teach' when testing. They found that they were being very directive in their questioning and were leading pupil responses. The APU team developed an approach in which they attempted to be relatively non-directive using prompts and probes to investigate pupil thinking. They found themselves offering encouragement to pupils to respond, rephrasing questions, focusing pupils' attention, prompting more reflective thinking and even asking simpler and more straightforward questions.

COMMUNICATION AND THE TEACHER

The role of teacher questioning has been examined from the perspective of sociological studies of classroom control. Edwards and Westgate (1987) and Mehan (1979) have suggested that teacher questioning may play a significant role in establishing and confirming the teacher's control over the lesson. Teachers may have an 'agenda' which guides the way they use the information elicited by their questions. In this context there are 'rules of the game' of question asking and answering that may seek to inhibit pupil responses. This may be particularly the case for pupils who have 'suffered at the hands' of a 'questions as control' regime. Too often, the teacher does not respond to incorrect solutions but waits for a correct one before continuing the lesson. Time taken to pursue incorrect responses may reveal misunderstandings shared by many pupils in the class. Too often, the single correct response appears to be the only one that matters.

The practice of rephrasing questions has received some support from the psychologist Hundeide (1985). He obtained evidence that children respond more positively to situations in which they are offered another person's interpretation of a problem rather than a direct question. Thus saying something like 'the way I see it is . . .' rather than 'what is . . .' is more likely to elicit a fruitful response. This finding accords with those of Schoenfeld (1985) on the public thinking through of problem solving as discussed in Chapters 3 and 4. There is an important distinction to be made here between 'explaining' and 'showing'. Schoenfeld showed his students how his own thought processes worked. He did not explain how they were supposed to think. Hundeide was also offering a tentative proposal rather than a definitive statement. Both writers were offering invitations to enter a dialogue rather than transmit a formal explanation.

An additional point is made by the CSMS team who also argue for a more dialogue-based, discursive model of mathematics teaching in the classroom:

> Talking to individual children may soon clear up certain misconceptions which the child will not voice in public. It was noticeable during the interviews, carried out as part of this research that children were learning simply by voicing their own thoughts.
>
> (Hart, 1981, p. 213)

It is not clear why the CSMS team feel that this process of 'learning through voicing' works. One explanation is that the pupils were bringing their learning under their own verbal control and that the process of questioning served to prompt a procedure which may be described as one of self-regulation.

LANGUAGE POLICY

Larcombe (1985) suggests that perhaps too much emphasis is laid on 'correct mathematical language' at the expense of working with the pupil's own language. Although he does not reference this concern to models of pedagogy it is clear that he is discussing one of the inherent consequences for the discourse of mathematics in a transmission-based pedagogy. As Larcombe notes it is all too easy for teachers to stifle 'the language and self expression of the learner by appearing to anticipate the language they should use rather than encouraging whatever language they do use' (p. 40). An important extension of this position is with respect to how the teacher proceeds from that of accepting pupil language whatever its nature, form and consequences. The constructivist answer in this case would be that it is important to establish the pupil's voice in a mathematical dialogue and then proceed to help the learner understand other ways of discussing the issue at hand. This marks a significant difference from the form of classroom practice which is content to accept 'unofficial' use of language as the only valid basis for discussion. Many of the constructivist writers reviewed in this book would suggest that it is the role of the teacher to connect the pupil's understanding (and thus language) with that of the wider world of mathematical practice. Thus instruction can take place and develop in a dialogue which is meaningful for all parties rather than instruction acting as some kind of pedagogic battering ram.

Accordingly Larcombe offers a number of suggestions for encouraging language use in the secondary mathematics classroom. Casting the teacher in the role of listener he recommends that pupils are encouraged to verbalize their thoughts, describe their actions and the objects and patterns with which they are operating.

Shuard and Rothery (1984) suggest that teachers identify and avoid the use of those aspects of Mathematical English which have become unnecessary (for example 'minuend'). In line with the Cockcroft Report they suggest using strategies such as repeated definitions, marginal comments, reminders, stronger context clues, a glossary and an index as ways of helping pupils to become familiar with and read technical terms. Although they make no theoretical justification of their position they present a strong plea for the inclusion of technical vocabulary in written texts. They argue that technical terms have an essential place in mathematics and that pupils cannot proceed without knowing them. They suggest that omitting technical words brings short-term advantages and long term difficulties. If pupils are not involved in using written and spoken terms they will face insuperable difficulties in making mathematical progress in school. Shuard and Rothery suggest four ways in which teachers can consider the use of particular words in written texts in mathematics. These provide useful guidelines when teachers or groups of teachers are involved in detailed forward planning of curriculum materials:

1. Is the word likely to be familiar to the reader?
2. In particular, is the reader likely to have met the Mathematical English words in mathematics lessons; do the Mathematical English words have everyday meanings which might cause confusion or cause a pupil to think in terms of a limited meaning?
3. Does a particular word appear in isolation or context?
4. Does the text have a good system of lexical familiarisation? (p. 31)

Shuard and Rothery also argue that the graphic displays and images used in mathematical texts present their own 'reading' demands. The conventions of the use of images may, rather than assisting the pupil to extract meaning, serve to compound confusion. They argue that whereas in a reading book a child may still be able to understand a story without understanding the implications of an illustration, in a mathematics text book failure to comprehend the significance of an illustration may be rather more serious. In the same way the significance of rhetorical questions is a source of confusion because pupils are not clear about the kind of response that they are expected to make to them. Similarly worked examples are rarely found to be enlightening by secondary school pupils.

In their work they suggest that it is difficult to provide simple formulae for identifying 'difficult' texts whether or not they contain symbols and illustrations. Their support is for informed teacher judgement in the evaluation of written materials in mathematics. They suggest a strategy for teachers to use when judging readability:

> First, the teacher should clearly identify the purpose of each of the different types of writing on the page, and then consider the small scale and large scale features contributing to readability. 'Small scale' features are vocabulary, syntax, symbols and details of diagrams. 'Large scale' features are those which affect the comprehension of the page or the pages as a whole: the flow of the meaning, layout of the page, and the interrelation of graphic material and the text. (p. 159)

Even with all the attention to the content and format of written mathematical texts advocated above it would seem that unless the whole language policy of mathematics is considered little progress will be achieved. Earp and Tanner (1980) found that the majority (93 per cent) of eleven-year-old pupils could mechanically read the words in their mathematics schemes but understood only about 50 per cent as evidenced in explanations or appropriate use. They argue that reading in mathematics is likely to be enhanced when children use the words which appear in the written texts in speech. They found that such speech was rare particularly in classrooms which made extensive use of schemes with large numbers of individual worksheets. This is precisely the kind of classroom context which concerned HMI (1989c). This problem may be exacerbated by the nature of the schemes provided for many of the pupils who are of concern here.

Dowling (1993) provides a powerful sociological critique of the way in which written language is used in the School Mathematics Project (SMP) Mathematics series. He examines the 'G' materials, directed at 'lower ability pupils' and the 'Y' scheme which represents the 'upper track' in the SMP eleven to sixteen scheme:

The two Teacher's Guides exhibit opposite positions. Within the 'G' scheme the teacher's role is to localise mathematics in respect of individual pupils and in respect of the local environment. Within the 'Y' scheme the teacher is to generalise. 'G' pupils are to have their respective individualities reflected back at them: 'Y' pupils are to be apprenticed into a specialised discourse. (p. 4, mimeo version)

Dowling points out that the design of these different routes through what is still one of the most popular maths schemes in the country carries with it significant mathematical implications. The implicit assumptions about the nature of the pupils are relayed in the form of the instructional texts and carry with them mathematical implications. If these schemes were to be used as only part of the mathematical diet of pupils in secondary schools then perhaps there would not be such a cause for concern. However, HMI (1991) point out they still tend to be used in isolation.

It is, perhaps, worth remembering the comment made in the Cockcroft Report (DES, 1982) on the role of written instruction in mathematics:

The ability to learn mathematics from the printed page is one which develops very slowly, so that even at the age of 16 there are few pupils who are able to learn satisfactorily from a textbook by themselves. (para. 312)

In summary, it would seem that for what may be termed sociological as well as psychological reasons it is important that pupils gain access to the language of mathematics in school. This is more difficult for some pupils than others. Some require teachers who attend to the specific consequences of their communication difficulties. All pupils need the support of teachers who recognize that the learning of school mathematics will be approached from the base provided by everyday mathematical understanding and strategies. New ways of thinking will arise as pupils connect and adapt the mathematics of school to their own store of informal mathematics and/or previous experience of school. Teachers can provide instruction and discussion that supports this mathematical development through teaching that is responsive rather than impositional. They can also make school learning more accessible through scrutiny of the content and format of worksheets and other texts. Care should be taken to consider the mathematical implications of imposing restrictions on the oral and written language of the classroom. The language of the mathematical text needs to be used and usable in mathematical discussion.

Special teaching?

Clearly there is much to be done by way of the development of an educationally sound pedagogic practice for all children. Following Bennett (1987) and Baroody and Hume (1991) it would seem reasonable to expect that the move to design an effective maths curriculum for students with SEN would significantly improve their mathematical attainment. There remains the question of whether a special pedagogy should exist for some categories of SEN. Do some special needs require special teaching? If so, how does this special teaching relate to what counts as 'mainstream' teaching? In this chapter we will attempt to explore these issues with respect to specific learning difficulties.

SPECIAL LEARNERS?

In the USA many pupils are said to experience 'learning disabilities'. Arguably this is a socially more acceptable experience than that of being said to be 'mentally retarded'. The concept of 'mathematical disability' is often promoted and associated with particular forms of instruction:

> Although many students with maths deficiencies exhibit characteristics that predispose them to maths disabilities (e.g. problems in memory, language, reading, reasoning and metacognition) their learning difficulties are often compounded by ineffective instruction. Many authorities [. . .] believe that poor or traditional instruction is a primary cause of the maths problems of many students with learning problems. Numerous studies support the position that students with maths disabilities can be taught to improve their mathematical performance [. . .].
>
> Given the poor math progress of students with learning problems and the call for a reform in maths education to increase standards, a need clearly exists to design an effective maths curriculum for these students.
>
> (Mercer and Miller, 1992, p. 20)

In a review of studies concerned with the relationship between education and intelligence, Snow and Yallow (1982) suggest that there is evidence of different needs for instruction. They conclude that children who experience difficulty in learning in mathematics benefit from practical activities, illustration, concrete examples and small-step teaching. However, they also state that the same educational activities may inhibit learning in the case of pupils who make good progress. They further argue that as successful pupils are involved in the process of inventing their own problem-solving procedures then teacher intervention may be counter-productive if it is not based on a clear understanding of the pupil's procedures. As we have argued these are often highly idiosyncratic and difficult to comprehend. The dilemma that exists here is with the respect to the amount of 'special' intervention that should be given. If 'bright' or 'normal' pupils are seen to need an amount of autonomy in problem solving should this be denied to pupils who experience difficulty in learning? Ahmed (1985, 1987) reporting the LAMP and RAMP projects argues against the denial of independence in mathematical learning for low-attaining pupils in secondary schools.

The term 'dyscalculia' is used to define such a supposedly special group who are mathematically 'disabled'. Austin (1982) reviews the literature and suggests that research provides very little guidance for the classroom teacher and attributes this to the imprecise definition of the term dyscalculia and the consequent diversity in the population to whom the term is applied. His conclusion argues in favour of the 'better pedagogy for all' position:

> If specific techniques of teaching arithmetic to learning disability children cannot be identified, then we need to study how effective are the usual methods with this population. (p. 207)

Miles and Miles (1992) find no evidence in favour of the existence of a mathematical specific learning difficulty beyond that which is often associated with the condition they define as dyslexia. These difficulties are addressed by Thomson (1991) who provides a table listing the problems facing the child with what he terms 'dyslexia' in mathematics classes:

Memory
1. Retention of tables.
2. Remembering of procedures and rules.
3. Retention of information while calculating (eg regrouping or addends).

Reading Reading the question, comprehension in problem solving, undertaking required operations.
1. Use of ruler, protractor and compass.
2. Cutting out.

3. Formation of numbers and letters.

Direction
1. Horizontal sequencing, i.e. from left to right.
2. Vertical sequencing, i.e. from bottom to top.
3. Confusion with x and + symbols.

Organisation
1. Sub-skills of the hierarchical system.
2. Order of the processes during calculation.

Perception
1. Concept labelling, i.e. symbols, names.
2. Complex relationships-place value.
3. Conservation is often a slow process (p. 193).

Even a casual inspection of this list would suggest that there is nothing exceptional about the range of these difficulties. Whilst, as Thomson notes, there is precious little research into mathematical learning in the group of children identified as dyslexic, it would seem reasonable to assume that many of the children so classified would experience these difficulties rather more often and intensely than many children not so classified.

However, the basic dilemma of need for structure versus need for independence and autonomy manifests itself in Thomson's recommendations for the teaching of pupils described as 'dyslexic':

1. The need for a fully structured teaching programme.
2. Expectations must be realistic.
3. Integrated approach to teaching tables using multisensory techniques similar to simultaneous oral spelling procedures.
4. Providing success in areas of strength.
5. Circumventing difficulties.
6. Rewarding correct responses.
7. Undertaking small sequential steps and recognising that there are many routes to the same objective. (pp. 195–6)

Again most of these suggestions would appear to be sensible from a 'common sense' point of view. As with so many sets of suggestions provided for teachers there is a dearth of guidance on how to implement such advice. In the absence of a strong research base it would appear that the insistence that 'one should start with basics and build up slowly to more complicated concepts', carries with it a number of problems. If a programme is to be structured where does the structure come from? The question as to who decides that which is basic is, of course, highly problematic. Reference to this issue in the context of the teaching of reading is sufficient reminder that the notion of 'basic' in complex learning is highly problematic. Research (Denvir, 1986) has shown that when mathematics learning is proposed as a hierarchy of developing inter-related skills and teaching is aimed at specific sub-skills to match absent skills in individual children, the learning outcome is not assured. A hierarchical framework may be useful for describing an individual's knowledge in mathematics but is often unreliable for predicting which cognitive skills the child is likely to learn next. Without control of the learning outcomes of teaching, a rich environment incorporating many possible outcomes must be favoured above one which is narrowly prescriptive in the mathematics presented.

Also as Parmar and Cawley (1991) remind their readers, structure can come to inhibit some forms of mathematical learning and render the learner passive. Similarly the suggestion that expectations must be realistic would seem to be in opposition to the more general movement within the SEN field which suggests that the social definition of 'realistic' is often a severe underestimate. It is difficult to achieve a balance between that which is accessible yet challenging and that which is de-motivating either through its complexity or its simplicity.

Following Snow and Yallow (1982) and much of the 'dyslexia' based literature there would appear to be a strong suggestion that some 'special' children need teaching that is special in that it is highly structured. Following Wood (1988) and Resnick and Ford (1981) it would seem that mathematical learning normally proceeds on the basis of individuals creating and developing their own strategies within the demands of instructional guidance. In this context too much structure in teaching is seen to inhibit progress. HMI reports provide a reminder that 'structure' often appears in the form of a single scheme of work cards, work sheets or set of books which are used in an unmodified form for whole groups of pupils. This situation may well be unsatisfactory for all. If some basic goals of mathematical education include items such as enabling pupils to become autonomous learners and enabling learners to develop strategies for solving a wide variety of problems in a wide variety of contexts with confidence, then appropriate means for achieving these ends are required. Whole class application of inflexible linear schemes would not appear to be appropriate means.

STRUCTURED PROGRAMMES OF STUDY

If many of the interventions being developed under the banner of 'constructivist approaches' offer a range of potential means of making progress for most pupils then one may ask – 'what becomes of the "special" pupil who "needs structure"?'. Perhaps the key questions become – what do they need 'structure' for and what kind of structure is required to meet these needs? If the first question is referenced to goals of autonomy, independence and flexibility then the answer to the second question is unlikely to be found in a system of teaching that renders pupils passive. The answer is more likely to be found in an approach that provides focused tasks designed to develop pupils' understanding and to engage with their own specific strategies and protocols. Hence the structure to some great extent would be special to the individual. It would be designed to enable the pupil to engage in 'mainstream' mathematical activity using strategies that had been developed in close collaboration with their teacher. The work of Resnick (1984) can be taken as support for this position. She considers the source of systematic errors in subtraction with multidigit numbers. She argues that conceptual misunderstandings lie at the heart of many erroneous procedures, and that these misunderstandings are what should be addressed in instruction.

One could imagine that programmes of study may be individualized to take account of pupil need through procedures such as those outlined in Stages 1 to 3 of the Code of Practice. They should be developed in consultation between the SEN staff and the mathematics staff. Above all any proposal for a particular form of structured teaching could be treated experimentally and be open for evaluation and review. This is a far cry from the more familiar type of individualized instruction which is based on a selection from a pregiven set of instructions which allow for differences in pace but not sequence or content. Instead, individual priorities could be used to formulate individual programmes on the basis of information gained through diagnostic and formative assessment and the kind of instructional dialogues typified by some forms of error analysis. These programmes would be designed to enable the individual pupils to participate in the kind of activities considered to be mathematically important for all pupils with negotiated progress and goals. This does not preclude the use of commercial schemes but requires thoughtful planning of the way such schemes may be supportive for individual needs.

There may well be some special issues which form a common set of concerns for many teachers working with pupils experiencing learning difficulties in secondary mathematics classrooms. Better access to research findings could come to act as prompts to teachers when they investigate a particular pupil's learning. Dockrell and McShane (1993) provide a review of some of the literature concerned with specific difficulties in number. They suggest, for example, that poor skills in counting underlie a number of difficulties with number. Citing Baroody (1986) and Fuson (1988) they argue that children with a moderate learning difficulty make matching errors at the beginning and end of counts and that the co-ordination and production of number words and pointing are major sources of difficulty. They make general recommendations which are based on a number of studies conducted within the rubric of cognitive psychology. They advocate the use of strategies which reduce demands on working memory resources, such as counting on fingers. Arguing that pupils can reason about number without being explicitly taught to do so, they suggest that when these skills are present in cases of number difficulty it makes sense to encourage the child to use them in problem solving. Further as the vast majority of errors in multidigit arithmetic involves operations on zero, they argue that assessment should attend to this explicitly:

> Children have a natural aptitude for number. They readily learn to count and to solve problems using counting. However, some children have difficulty in learning to count. Number problems start here. If they are not overcome, then they can lead to a vicious circle in the acquisition of more advanced arithmetical skills that rely on counting for their establishment.
>
> Children with basic number problems differ from their peers in their ability to use number strategies effectively and efficiently. They often continue to employ inefficient and time consuming strategies when their peers have advanced to more efficient strategies. Their own perception of their inefficiency can be discouraging to these children leading them to lose interest in mathematics. (p. 146)

Clearly there is a need to avoid exchanging one sort of 'vicious circle' for another. The 'vicious circle' of inefficient counting strategies must not be replaced by an instructional 'vicious circle' of stultifying and meaningless repetitions of inappropriate tasks which remain in blissful isolation from the point of real contact that is needed. Structured learning programmes will involve informed teachers and responsive pupils in planning long and short term tasks with identified outcomes and productive extensions where appropriate.

There are three matters of priority invoked in this kind of approach. The first is that all teacher intervention should be designed to facilitate participation in 'real' mathematics. This priority affirms the need to ensure that pupils are not rendered mathematically passive by a system of drill and practice driven worksheets. The second matter of priority is that structured intervention should be informed by the findings of research and the existing mathematical strategies possessed by the pupil even if it seeks to change these. An instructional connection must be made between pupil understanding and the relevant mathematical goals in the classroom. Thirdly, an attempt should be made to identify the most important obstacles to learning. This priority recognizes that time for detailed and properly planned SEN intervention which is genuinely responsive to need is a very limited resource. Time is needed for teachers to come to understand where difficulties are seated. Then mathematics teaching becomes a learning exercise for the teachers as well as the pupils.

NEEDS OF SPECIAL NEEDS TEACHERS

One of the major problems with the reform of mathematics teaching has been the process of implementation and thus by implication professional development for teachers. It is ironic that within a system that spends so much time considering how young people think and learn that the development of teachers is too often forgotten. Just as we have argued that pupils do not adopt procedures rather that they adapt them it would seem sensible to posit the same processes in the professional development of teachers.

The issue of the emotional impact of mathematical difficulty referenced by Dockrell and McShane (1993) and given a full consideration by Buxton (1981) is discussed in terms of teacher characteristics by Macnab and Cummine (1986):

> At the heart of the constructivist approach is a sensitivity on the part of the teacher to be able feel as the learner feels, to put himself in the learner's shoes, not only in the cognitive sense, but also in the emotional sense. The mathematical misconceptions of many children may often be beyond our grasp; that there are such misconceptions born out of anxiety and confusion which disastrously affect the learning process should never be forgotten. (p. 39)

Discussions of special needs practices in schools sometimes appear somewhat technical. The use of particular forms of what is often, perhaps rightly, called 'psychobabble' may leave a reader with the impression that an almost clinical task is at hand. However as Macnab and Cummine rightly point out the nature of the teacher is at least of as much importance as the nature of any teaching content. In their view good teachers may be seen to exhibit the following characteristics:

- They cultivate with pupils relationships of encouragement and emotional warmth. Encouragement can be rarely overdone;
- They maintain, and are seen to maintain, a liking for and interest and involvement in mathematics;
- They seek a develop self-achievement in pupils through a pattern of activities in which such self-achievement is possible;
- They discuss mathematics with their pupils rather simply transmit it, so that pupils can come to distinguish between mathematical fact and notational convenience and practice and, more generally, achieve a greater awareness of the process of mathematical development. (p. 18)

Peterson, Fennema and Carpenter (1989) suggest that although there is now a sizeable body of knowledge on the psychology of children's classroom learning of mathematics it would seem that even experienced teachers do not have access to it. In part their research team attribute this to the way in which research traditions themselves have developed.

> Previously, researchers studying teaching had focused on staff development and/or instruction and teacher's cognitions during instruction, but generally had not been concerned with children's learning of mathematics. In contrast, researchers on children's cognitions had been concerned with what was learned, but for the most part not addressed the question of how it was facilitated.
>
> (Peterson *et al.*, 1989, p. 556)

They studied the impact of training teachers in what they term 'Cognitively Guided Instruction'. Rather than training them in specific techniques for instruction the teachers participated in a four week workshop at which recent findings on children's learning and cognition were presented. They studied teachers' cognitions and their teaching as they interact with use of knowledge about children's mathematical thinking in making instructional decisions. In comparison with a control group these teachers showed more agreement with the following statements:

1. Children construct their own mathematical knowledge.
2. Mathematics instruction should be organised to facilitate children's construction of knowledge.
3. Children's development of mathematical ideas should provide the basis for sequencing topics for instruction.
4. Mathematical skills should be taught in relation to understanding and problem solving.

> (Peterson *et al.*, 1989, p. 45)

Thus through the updating of teachers own knowledge of the mathematical learning process they appeared to affiliate to some of the elements of a constructivist approach. Peterson *et al.* found that as a consequence of this updating of their knowledge base these teachers also changed their classroom practice:

> The process of teacher change, although dependent on student outcomes, is usually an interactive one. When children begin to show increased learning, teachers continue to implement new methodologies that result in improved learning, and so the circle continues.
>
> (Peterson *et al.*, 1989, p. 580)

It should be noted that this work was carried out with serving teachers. There is substantial evidence that the situation may be somewhat different in Initial Teacher Training. Most recently

Eisenhart *et al.* (1993) report that trainee teachers seem to be in need of initial teaching practice in classroom environments which themselves confirm and are congruent with the practices announced in training. The all too familiar pattern of reversion to past personal experience as a learner for information as to how to teach is a consequence of not attending to the formative role of the teaching practice environment. Serving teachers practice may be enhanced as they benefit from updates about the way in which children think and learn if they are then able to apply teaching approaches that make a difference. Novice teachers need to be placed in teaching environments which support the practices put forward in training.

There have been many successes in the integration of pupils with special needs into the mainstream mathematics classroom but further development is necessary if the identified difficulties are to be addressed and every individual given their right to a comprehensive education in mathematics. Fleming *et al.* report on the practical implications of operating a support system from the subject teacher's perspective and conclude that 'all teachers can become successful teachers of children with special needs' and the following would be helpful to develop the system already established in school:

- Some in-service training or advisory support in order to develop or acquire a more thorough knowledge of the nature of learning difficulties and the development of mathematical concepts. In addition knowledge of more diagnostic assessment material which would enable more detailed specific help to be given to individual children.
- Some time, money and help in developing practical activities.
- Some in-service training in the use of number apparatus with children with severe problems.

(from Fleming et al., 1990)

This list is far from comprehensive but identifies the needs expressed by teachers and would fruitfully form the basis for investment in research and for in-service training of teachers.

Rather than training 'special teachers' with 'special skills' to teach 'special pupils' it would seem that the needs of most teachers of pupils with SEN are likely to be met through school and departmental support in INSET that is designed to foster responsive teaching that is not constricted by the gaze of categories which serve administrative rather than pedagogic purposes.

In summary, in this chapter we have discussed two major issues:

1. The dilemma that exists with respect to pedagogic control within the curriculum.
2. The needs of the teachers who teach children with special needs.

Our intention has been to provide a cost/benefit analysis of the procedures which invoke the development of a highly-controlled, special curriculum. We suggest that there is at the very best, limited evidence to support the case for specific mathematical disability; that many of the forms of intervention which are said to be beneficial for this supposed group may in fact compound their difficulties and that the practice of restricting the mathematical activity of pupils to the confines of some of the highly-structured programmes that exist may in fact be 'disabling' in itself.

We have advanced the proposal that special teaching should be characterized in terms of the extent to which it is responsive to the needs of the learner and that this implies the need to 'tune in' to pupil strategies rather than apply a uniform 'remedial curriculum blanket'. With the thought in mind that many such 'blankets' may act more to provide a sense of security for teachers rather than meeting the instructional needs of pupils, we discuss the characteristics of the teachers that we suggest are required to meet the special needs of pupils. Given appropriate support and training we argue that significant improvements may be made in schools for pupils with SEN. Within schools, opportunities for collaboration between teachers of mathematics and SEN support staff can become part of a planned programme for meeting the needs of individual pupils. We address some of the institutional implications in the next chapter.

—8—

School implications

This chapter will explore the implications of the previous chapters for aspects of whole-school policy development and action as against that which is specific to a particular classroom. If we adopt the position that it is difficult, if not impossible (and perhaps unhelpful), to impose a rigid distinction between that which is 'special' and that which is 'ordinary' within a mainstream school, then integration becomes a matter of generating a model of organization sufficiently flexible to meet the pedagogic demands of a continuum of learning needs. This is particularly relevant for the mathematics classroom where confidence may be lacking in a range of low-attaining children whose needs have to be individually addressed. In curricular terms this becomes a matter of ensuring that pupils are assured access to their curriculum entitlements in such a way as they may demonstrate their existing competencies and make as much progress as possible. In practice this is far from easy.

The twin strategies of whole-school policy development and individual support intervention are familiar in many secondary schools. The process of curriculum differentiation is a more recent entry into the priorities of secondary school managers (see Weston *et al.*, 1992) where entitlement to a Programme of Study at an appropriate level has become a statutory requirement of the National Curriculum. Considerations of whole-school policy development, individual support work and the process of curriculum differentiation will now be reviewed from the perspective of mathematics teaching. A section of this chapter is also devoted to issues of discrimination and bias which are clearly matters for whole-school policy development.

ASPECTS OF WHOLE-SCHOOL POLICY

Schools are now required to describe the way in which they make provision for children who are considered to have SEN. The Code of Practice requires that schools provide parents with details of their arrangements for children with SEN:

- on the school's policy;
- on the support available for children with SEN within the school and LEA;
- on parents' rights to be involved in assessment and decision making emphasizing the importance of their contribution;
- on services such as those provided by the local authority for children in need;
- on local and national voluntary organisations which might provide information, advice or counselling.

(from DFE, 1994)

They are also required to develop and maintain partnership and access arrangements with parents. Schools have also been asked to consider how they will involve pupils in SEN assessment and intervention. Schools should consider how they:

- involve pupils in decision making processes;
- determine the child's level of participation, taking into account approaches to assessment and intervention which are suitable for his or her age, ability and past experiences;
- record pupils' views in identifying their difficulties, setting goals, agreeing a development strategy, monitoring and reviewing progress;
- involve pupils in implementing individual education plans.

(from DFE, 1994)

These new official requirements bring matters of policy development in SEN work to the attention of school managers if for no other reason than that they will be scrutinized in OFSTED inspections. There will, of course, be considerable variation in the extent to which schools become involved in real policy development as against what might be termed 'policy production'. The benefits for a school that does make a whole-hearted commitment to active policy development are likely to be considerable as the process is much more likely to result in practices which enhance the performance of the school. Within the purchaser/provider model espoused by the Audit Commission (HMI, 1992), Special Provision is seen to compliment mainstream provision and thus schools will need to be in a position to audit their existing skills and resources and be able to articulate the nature of the provision that they offer or can offer in partnership with other schools.

As HMI noted in their report on Special Needs and the National Curriculum 1991–92:

Schools . . . should review and monitor their curriculum to assess how well it provides the access for pupils with special needs required by the 1988 Education Act. [They] . . . need to conduct a thorough audit of

provision of books and teaching materials for pupils with special educational needs, and to improve it since, in a significant number of schools,
inadequate provision presents obstacles to pupils' progress in some subjects; work could be more closely matched to pupils' abilities.

(from HMI, 1993)

School mathematics provision usually involves a commercial scheme
which may or may not be adapted to be suitable for a range of
abilities. In practice, *ad hoc* arrangements centred on specially produced worksheets often form the basis of instruction for many special
needs children. At best, a commercial scheme supplemented with
additional materials may provide a structured curriculum of selected
tasks, supported with practical activities involving appropriate
resources. At worst, some children experience no more than a series
of 'one off' pencil and paper problem sheets whose relevance are
poorly or never understood by the children.

Collaboration between schools

A shortcoming of the individual school approach is that the range of
expertise needed to address all special needs may not be found in one
school. Dyson and Gains (1993) suggest that schools should begin
exploring collaborative partnerships with other schools and services
in order to supplement what they can provide internally. They argue
for a model of collaboration which in many ways echoes the European
notion of subsidiarity that is a decentralized organization of responsibilities, with the aim of never entrusting to a larger unit what can
better be realized by a smaller one. In school terms this means that
the organization is such that teachers and departments are account-
able for agreed approaches to SEN:

Schools will have to organise themselves internally so that each
classroom, like each school, is the locus of a range of educational services flexibly delivered, which secure effective learning for all students.
(p. 168)

HMI in their report on the integration of MLD pupils into mainstream
schools suggest that secondary mainstream schools could engage in
a number of institutional strategies in order to facilitate the development of an educationally responsive system:

- join with special schools in the development of guidelines to prepare
  pupils for integration;
- set up joint liaison and review systems to ensure continuing support
  and monitoring of progress;
- involve the senior management team and governors;
- develop or strengthen curricular links with special schools;

- encourage fully and partially integrated pupils to take part in extra-curricular activities to foster social relationships.

(from HMI, 1993)

These suggestions are very much in sympathy with the notions of autonomous actions within strategic plans envisaged by Dyson and Gains. They discuss autonomy in terms of teachers and schools with devolved powers and resources responding as problem solvers to their own situations. This autonomy is embedded in patterns of strategic control in which some management system within or outside the school, beyond the individual teacher and individual school is charged with setting the parameters of the problems to be solved, with devolving responsibilities and resources, and with monitoring outcomes, (Dyson and Gains, 1993). Strength in mathematical provision will come from sharing ideas and experiences within school and through the establishment of a local group with a special needs focus.

Within the school this approach calls on the mathematics department to develop policies and procedures for collaborating with other departments within the school and agencies outside the school. These structures for collaboration should provide a mechanism whereby relevant aspects of school SEN policy are actually implemented at the classroom level within departments. Strategies for achieving this will, of course, vary as a function of the cultural/micro-political context of the school. Stradling and Saunders (1993) suggest that the SEN co-ordinator may well come to develop important whole-school policy development roles in the future. They suggest a model of different levels of support for policy development with an implicit model of progression:

The SEN co-ordinator may

1. Make *ad hoc* arrangements with individual teachers.
2. Make links with individual departments through such colleagues.
3. Work with departmental deputies to create a differentiation team working across the school.
4. Work with the whole staff to broaden the range of teaching/learning styles for all pupils. (p. 136)

The Code of Practice for SEN work places a heavy burden of responsibility on SEN co-ordinators. Strategies such as the one outlined above could prove to be invaluable to SEN co-ordinators as they attempt to implement the Code. Responsibilities will be shared with the Head of Mathematics whose approach to Special Needs provision will find much in common with actions for all low attainers in mathematics. Actions suggested in the Mathematical Association's *Managing Mathematics: Handbook for the Head of Department* (1988) are the following:

(i) Review current prevalence of and provision for low attainers in the school and department. (E.g. does a special needs teacher look after mathematics along with other subjects? What kind of communication (regarding low attainers) is there between departments?)

(ii) What kind of status does work with low attainers have in the department? What kind of resources are devoted to it – both in quantity and nature? (e.g. are practical materials available for appropriate practical work?)

(iii) Is there a need for a specialist co-ordinator of such work in the department? Could that person be most effective by working alongside other members of the department while providing additional help for particular pupils? Will that person benefit from attending an appropriate in-service course?

(iv) What form of in-service training within school can help all staff develop their skills further?

(v) What form of local advice/support is available – at a teachers' centre, from an advisory teacher (or among the local consortium of schools)?

(vi) Review the curriculum in terms of the content. (Does it go beyond computation? Are topics developed to a point where pupils see some purpose?) and the teaching approach. (Is class teaching appropriate? What is the place of practical work projects?)

(vii) Establish a resource bank of appropriate materials and a library of ideas and case studies. (p. 38)

In many schools, case studies form the basis for discussion between mathematics and special needs staff. A department policy must extend beyond these necessary discussions and work towards the establishment and regular review of provisions across all special needs. A portfolio of case studies and the activities that proved to be most successful may be included among the resources available. Fleming, Dadswell and Dodgson suggest that 'all teachers can become successful teachers of children with special educational needs, and that children can be successfully supported in the mainstream classroom'. They identify certain features as contributors to success:

(a) Clear specification of roles and responsibilities.

(b) Provision of differentiated resources which enable children to work at their individual level.

(c) The meticulous organization of material resources.

(d) A deliberate policy of protection of the support teacher when cover is needed.

(e) The status given to support teaching by the head of department and second in department adopting the role.

(f) Regular meetings to plan and evaluate the provision: regular and honest interaction can prevent a minor irritation from becoming a major crisis.

(g) A comprehensive record keeping system.

(h) Staff who are willing to adapt to each other's needs and the needs of the system.

(i) Classrooms which are close together.

(from Fleming et al., 1990)

It is clear that these actions will not be sufficient for those special needs children who are not low attainers and provision for individual needs must extend beyond the 'bottom sets' in mathematics. Identification and implementation of appropriate support strategies can result in departmentally shared responsibilities for special needs children and better opportunity for each individual child to have access to a mathematics programme of study at a level which is both challenging and rewarding.

TEACHER SUPPORT TEAMS

One form of indirect provision that has yet to receive much attention in secondary schools is direct support for teachers themselves. Teacher support teams (TSTs) are school-based interventions designed to help teachers be more effective at solving and coping with teaching problems presented by pupils. They act as problem-solving groups based in schools which support pupils indirectly through teacher collaboration. Staff request collaborative support from teams to understand problems and design appropriate forms of intervention related to learning and behaviour difficulties. This form of organizational response is at present under scrutiny in a number of primary schools (Daniels and Norwich, 1993; Daniels *et al.*, 1993).

Experience from the USA has shown that children with difficulties in learning are likely to benefit from teaching which derives from joint collaboration between teachers. When class teachers seek assistance for children presenting learning and behaviour difficulties, they can benefit from collaborating with colleagues who understand their particular circumstances. Teams can provide moral support to teachers, by helping teachers to realize that they are not alone and that others have similar difficulties. Teams also provide teachers who find some children's behaviour disturbing with an opportunity to air their frustrations.

In this country there has been surprisingly little use made of them. One possible reason is the often found culture of schools, which encourages a conception of the teacher as isolated in the classroom with no established system of peer collaboration. Teacher support teams represent a significant way of establishing peer support which is compatible with professional autonomy. Professional autonomy would be well served by schools having a system of collegial assistance in response to voluntary requests for assistance. Team meetings provide a forum for teachers to share their knowledge and know-how with each other in a context which is supportive and non-judgmental. In providing a structured and accessible forum for encouraging an interchange between peers in connection with specific teaching difficulties, support teams can contribute to making schools more effective. In this way TSTs become an intermediary form of provision between individual, child-focused, support arrangements and whole-school policy initiatives.

Teacher support teams could play a significant part at an early stage in the SEN referral systems by enhancing the school's own resources of expertise through this type of teacher collaboration. They could also be a very useful system for schools to offer more effective provision for children with special educational needs in the context of Local Management of Schools. The data from the evaluation of TST work in primary schools suggest that TSTs enhance the role of the SEN Co-ordinator and may also provide a way in which the implementation Code of Practice may be facilitated (Daniels *et al.*, 1993)

SPECIAL TEACHERS

The most common form of resource for special needs in secondary schools involves part-time and full-time staff in a team or as individuals. Links between the mathematics department and staff concerned with special needs vary widely from school to school and continuity of appropriate provision will depend on a pattern of liaison that can be sustained within the demands made on both mathematics and special needs staff. Where there is a separate department for special needs, or indeed among individuals, it is unusual to find teachers well qualified in mathematics. Collaborative planning utilizing the unique and useful contributions of all staff in a balanced programme will need extra effort if provision for pupils is to be adequate. Particular attention to the needs of part-time staff would seem to be important. As HMI (1991) report, part-time staff are often not involved enough in planning meetings to deliver the National Curriculum and in some schools this will need remedying as a first step to improving provision.

DIFFERENTIATION

The rhetoric of many recent initiatives has tended to dwell on the development of a broad and balanced curriculum which is sufficiently differentiated to allow all children to have access to their educational entitlements. However, as the NCC noted in 1990, Key Stage 3 of the National Curriculum presents significant challenges to schools in 'accommodating differences in children's abilities, aptitudes and needs', particularly in Mathematics and Science. This section will discuss the whole-school issues involved in moving towards a differentiated curriculum. In doing so it will necessarily need to make reference to what are seen to be current models and practices of curriculum differentiation.

The very word 'differentiation' appears to have entered the discourse of schooling in the guise of some kind of latter-day pedagogic saviour. It would seem that provided the magic word 'differentiation' is in action then problems associated with the implementation of the National Curriculum with SEN work, indeed with almost everything, will be solved. The actual nature of the 'magic' is as one would expect, not altogether clear. Gary Thomas suggests that the use of the word should be abandoned as it only serves to provide a reassuring gloss over complex issues:

> Differentiation implies that there is some kind of received process through which teachers can pass to enable them to make what is being taught comprehensible to all children. The jargon smoothes over the messiness of real classroom life. The phenomenally difficult process of making learning come alive for all children is reduced to a single, flat, abstract noun. By its use, the complexity, the difficulty, of that process is denied.
>
> (from Thomas, 1993)

The definition of differentiation offered by the Low Attaining Pupils Project team implicitly announces the key curriculum control issue when individual needs are being considered:

> Differentiation is therefore seen as the process of identifying, with each learner, the most effective strategies for achieving agreed targets.
> (from Stradling *et al.*, 1991)

In that the definition refers to the process of reaching agreement with a learner it suggests some kind of pedagogic dialogue in which the learner has a voice. This notion accords with some elements of the constructivist approach discussed in Chapter 3. If differentiation carries with it such a whole-scale pedagogic reform as is implied by a move towards the implementation of a constructivist paradigm then surely Thomas is right when he suggests that this is going to be a messy process. There would appear to be considerable resistance to the introduction of a more dialogic pedagogy.

On the one hand the Non-Statutory Guidelines in mathematics advocate a pedagogy which is responsive to individuals:

> Progression is to do with the ways in which teachers and pupils together explore, make sense of and construct pathways through the network of ideas that is mathematics. Each person's map of the network and of the pathways connecting mathematical ideas is different, thus people understand mathematics in different ways. The teacher's job is to organise and provide the sorts of experiences which enable pupils to construct and develop their own understanding of mathematics rather than simply communicate the ways in which they understand mathematics themselves.
>
> (DES, 1989b, C1)

In practice, however, HMI (1991) present a picture of teaching in schools in which there is great confusion and uncertainty about 'what to do' and 'how to do it' with respect to the teaching of new mathematics content in the curriculum for children with learning difficulties (Daniels, 1993b):

> Many schools used a commercial mathematics scheme, and while they were often valuable in providing a structure for mathematics courses there was undue reliance on them in most schools. The consequences included a lack of differentiation; mathematics learning based on 'texts' with pupils simply carrying out step-by-step instructions rather than on 'contexts'; restricted mathematical thinking; and poorly developed understanding.
>
> (HMI, 1991, p. 22)

Thus whilst the advice is cast in terms of diversity of instructional need much of the practice is predicated upon implicit assumptions of uniformity. The way in which the National Curriculum is being implemented suggests that an overemphasis on attainment predominates.

Despite all the changes which have taken place in the structure and content of the educational system it would seem that much remains the same when viewed from the perspective of the child with learning difficulties as reported by HMI in their survey of the practice of implementation of Key Stages 1 and 3 of the National Curriculum in Mathematics. In secondary schools many of the teachers who work with low-attaining pupils are seen to be in need of more help and support in the preparation of their teaching. Perhaps as a consequence of a more general lack of confidence, schools were seen to be using materials in a way that is unlikely to be supportive of the individual differences in approaches to learning mathematics. Most schools in the HMI survey relied too heavily on commercial mathematics schemes which were used in a largely undifferentiated way. As a consequence HMI noted:

> a lack of differentiation; mathematics learning based on 'texts' with pupils simply carrying out step-by-step instructions rather than on 'contexts'; restricted mathematical thinking; and poorly developed understanding. (p. 22)

Added to this many schools appear to feel that either they have already implemented the new mathematics system or only pay partial attention to the new demands facing them. Difficulty was noted with respect to some of the more innovative aspects of the curriculum. Ironically those items which appear to cause concern in schools are those items often put forward as being appropriate for children with learning difficulties:

> Many schools had difficulties with ATs 1 and 9 which are concerned with the processes of using and applying mathematics, because there had been little emphasis on these areas in the past. It was generally considered easier to fill 'content gaps' than to develop a mathematics curriculum in which these ATs underpinned all the mathematical work done by the pupils. As these ATs relate to all others, they place problem-solving, investigative activities and practical work at the centre of the mathematics curriculum ... [In schools] many of these changes were still 'bolt-on-extras' rather than integral parts of the curriculum. (pp. 15–16)

> A major challenge was to provide a mathematics curriculum for low-achieving pupils which was sound and balanced across all the ATs and not restricted to number and measures.
>
> (Williams, 1990)

The plea for breadth, balance and differentiation has been made in the context of what was regarded by many commentators as impoverished curriculum when viewed from the perspective of children who experience difficulty in learning mathematics. It may have been that within the world of SEN education the teaching of reading has occupied the gaze of the teacher almost to the exclusion of mathematics.

Stradling *et al.* (1991) employed the distinction of differentiation between groups and differentiation between individual learners. Quite clearly much of the practice witnessed by HMI was informed by the former rather than the latter. Differentiation in many of the situations observed arises by outcome rather than by task or means of engaging with the task. There is also the suggestion that the progression through a set of tasks within a scheme of work has been imposed and is not in a form whereby it meets even the specification of the common task within the definition of differentiation in the GCSE Guidelines (DES, 1985):

The setting of different tasks at different levels of difficulty – these must be suitable for different levels of achievement or it allows us to set common tasks that can be answered in a positive way by all pupils.

The consequences for the learner with SEN within the practices observed by HMI (1991) would seem to be all too clear. If differentiation is by outcome through a linear progression of tasks then some, maybe many, children will be cast into the role of the straggling low attainer. Such children may have their needs ignored in terms of tasks that they may either engage with and/or which take account of their needs for individual learning pathways to progress. Clearly this situation may be compounded by inappropriate design of a wide range of other procedures whether they be in terms of classroom management or prescribed modes of response. It seems more than possible that the National Curriculum is being implemented in a way that relays an expression of presumed homogeneity in pedagogic need. The assumption that all children think and learn in the same way and thus require teaching in exactly the same way is not without its detractors.

It would also seem that the planning process itself has retained an undue focus on narrowly defined outcomes at the expense of contexts for learning. This preoccupation with outcome expresses itself in teacher behaviour and carries consequences for pupil learning. The phrase 'new wine in old bottles' comes to mind. If, as HMI suggest, the process of curriculum reform in mathematics is doing little to subvert old pedagogic ideologies then all we are witnessing are changes in the *description* of the curriculum rather than in its practice.

Stradling and Saunders (1993) pose three questions which they feel that any school reviewing its policy on differentiation must face. Above all they argue that differentiation should be pedagogical rather than organizationally motivated:

1. Can [pupil] differences in attainment and/or learning capacity be adequately met by grouping pupils according to ability or past performance, whether general or subject related?
2. Will differentiation necessarily lead to teaching different curricula to different pupils, whether in groups or individually?
3. Or can differentiation be better realised through teaching the same curriculum to all pupils but tailoring the teaching approaches and processes to the different learning needs of pupils? (p. 129)

They offer a taxonomy of approaches to differentiation which they suggest can come to function as a menu from which schools can select their own priorities. The caution that priorities for differentiation ought to reflect the needs of learners rather than teachers is appended to the list:

1. By task – the same content in different levels.
2. By outcome – same general tasks which allow pupils to work and achieve at their own levels.
3. By learning activity – that pupils be allowed to engage with same content and tasks in different ways.
4. By pace or rate of learning.
5. By dialogue – teachers negotiate changes in work on the basis of changes in learning needs. (p. 130)

Implicit in this list is also the notion of differentiation in the criteria of evaluation, along with modes of communication and response. Associated with this understanding that differentiation is an active process comes the need for reliable information on approaches that have proved to be successful with particular pupils.

In terms of school-based strategies for differentiation Stradling *et al.* (1991) distinguish between targeted (alternative curriculum for a selected group of pupils focusing on a distinct aspect of provision) and dispersed differentiation strategies (invokes organizational curricular pedagogic changes). It is clear that schools have to decide on the extent to which they will attempt to implement the National Curriculum in a way that is responsive to individual learning needs. It is also clear that this decision is not entirely a curriculum matter in that it will be influenced by the organizational constraints generated by institutional needs. Thus the exact balance of targeted and dispersed strategies adopted in a particular school will to some extent reflect the outcome of cost/benefit analysis based on local constraints and incentives. It would seem wise that whenever a schools seeks to adopt a particular strategy on differentiation it is mindful of the fact that the process of implementation may take some considerable time. Particularly during the early phases of reform it would seem important to ensure that the 'costs' of change do not weigh too heavily on the most vulnerable learners in a school.

According to the NCC (1993) teachers reject the negative concept of disapplication and request this be replaced by a more positive approach to access to the National Curriculum. However, if, as HMI (1991) imply, the discourse of curriculum development is grounded in terms of attainment and Attainment Targets then there is every reason to believe that the process of differentiation will also be referenced to attainment. If differentiation is by school, set, stream, or group, schools or other groupings of narrow band attainment pupils could be formed as, supposedly, ideal sites for the efficient use of particular forms of instruction. This form of differentiation removes the economically unfortunate 'messiness' of the learning *process*.

Setting

There is some anecdotal evidence of an increase in the level of discussion of the topic of streaming in secondary schools and specific evidence that streaming in primary schools is being considered for subjects like mathematics. Some secondary schools are reportedly considering a return to fast streaming with a foreshortened pathway to the completion of Key Stages 3 and 4 perhaps encouraged by political intervention to identify and 'reward' the exceptionally able pupils with a supergrade in examinations. Whatever pattern of organizational arrangement a school adopts there would appear to be an important matter of the values which drive the system of resource allocation and priority associated with sets, streams and groups. HMI report mixed blessings for a variety of patterns of organization. The major issue seems to be with respect to the perceived value of teaching children who experience difficulty in learning.

HMI observed that low-ability sets, where well taught by specialists with understanding of SEN, had some advantages for pupils integrated from MLD schools in that class sizes were small and they were likely to be amongst the abler in the group. However, such sets were disadvantageous if the behaviour was poor or if they were taught by non-specialist teachers. Thus the priorities for the allocation of resources to teaching may have an impact on the quality of teaching and learning which is not always made explicit in schools:

> Where pupils were taught by teachers interested in them and with work prepared to meet their needs, they were secure, confident, well behaved and achieved encouraging standards. If low ability groups were taught by specialists with neither expertise nor insight into SEN and the work was not planned or matched to their needs, the quality of their work was poor and achievements were minimal.
>
> (from HMI, 1993)

HMI also noted that setting arrangements, and withdrawal provision for pupils with SEN are often perceived by special schools as more helpful than mixed-ability classes when integrating pupils. They suggest that such arrangements are likely to reduce the amount of additional support needed but may have some disadvantages for individual pupils. For example, withdrawal provision, if occurring for most of a pupil's time, can reduce integration both in curricular and social terms to something little more than locational integration. The lowest ability sets are frequently those with a higher proportion of pupils with behaviour problems, and this adds to the difficulties of newly integrated pupils. Crucially they observe that if a pupil moves to a school with a department for SEN that, in the main, operates a withdrawal system of classes or unit provision, the curriculum can sometimes be more limited than in the special school. In particular, work in English and Mathematics may be much narrower in its range than that received by peers outside the withdrawal classes. Sadly they noted that standards were particularly low in mathematics. Teachers will also be aware that 'promotion' to a higher set where support is not so readily forthcoming will disadvantage children's progress even where their potential is recognized to be beyond that of the rest of the group. How to provide for a potentially more able child without the de-stabilizing effect of changing set can become a real problem for successful teachers of low attainers.

It is perhaps worth remembering the comments of Brennan on the social implications of separating off groups of pupils into particular groupings whether on a curriculum or organizational basis:

> If the curriculum is to be differentiated in order to meet any special needs of slow learners then at what point (if any) does the differentiation become a separatist device, in that it cuts off the slow learner from the common aspects of the curriculum which contribute to cultural and social cohesion in our society.
>
> (from Brennan, 1979)

The management of groupings within a school is perhaps best driven by explicit reference to the value structure of the school. If all pupils are to be held in equal esteem then whatever organizational model of pupil organization is adopted care must be taken to ensure that these values are expressed in practical arrangements.

SUPPORT WORK

The experience of the implementation of the 1981 Act has shown that the move from patterns of full-time and part-time permanent or temporary withdrawal from mainstream classes towards greater support within the classroom was only successful when teachers collaborated in teaching, planning and reviewing lessons. In turn these acts of co-operation were invariably most successful in schools which had developed and maintained whole-school policies on special educational needs. The term 'support' became widely used and also developed many meanings. Support for teachers, support for schools, support for systems and support for children were all developed and often confused with one another. Swann notes that although support teachers have begun to see themselves as agents of curriculum change they have often been frustrated in their efforts:

> In some cases they have found themselves acting mainly as teaching aides with no control or influence of lesson content and methods and able to do little more than supervise and interpret for some pupils.
>
> (from Swann, 1988)

Subsumed in the notion of support is the understanding that it is worthwhile enabling children to have access to whatever experiences are being provided within the school. In terms of the 1988 Act, where support was offered from outside the school either by specialist services or other schools, the question has now become one of who will pay for these forms of co-operation in the era of local financial management of schools.

HMI (1993) have observed that teachers appointed to help individual pupils for a set number of hours per week are not always well used though they sometimes help to reduce behaviour problems. Most effective in-class support is that provided by an effective department for SEN using its specialist staff, rather than by teachers from other departments with spare periods. Additional support provided by a special support assistant is sometimes wasted, whereas when it is planned and co-ordinated in ways that integrate both the work of the mathematics teacher and the aims of the special needs teacher, the benefits to the pupils can be enormous (OFSTED, 1993b)

The effectiveness of in-class support is clearly linked to the willingness of mathematics teachers to collaborate with support teachers and also to engage with the children when the support teacher is not available. The finite amount of support time available from within the school's own resources to teachers and children in mainstream secondary schools is increasingly limited in the face of the effects of National Curriculum staffing demands. Support teams and services maintained by local authorities which in the past have done much to supplement the work of schools have been reduced in scale and scope. As a consequence exclusions and referrals for special provision have risen.

Dyson and Gains (1993) argue that there are at least two sets of implications for special needs teachers arising from the current changes in schooling. These involve both increasing generalization and specialization. Some special needs teachers will develop specific expertise in a way that does not simply replicate good generalist teaching. In the case of mathematics it may be that a cluster of schools may be able to fund and mutually benefit from the activities of a SEN support teacher who has developed specific expertise in mathematics. This person would then offer expertise in direct teaching and advice to teachers in classrooms. Their specific understanding of the pedagogic implications of particular aspects of the content of the curriculum would support the development of practical supplementary and complimentary teaching which would enhance the general curriculum menu in the classroom for all. This would also help to avoid the oft-heard anxiety expressed by SEN support teachers that they themselves feel insecure in specific lessons. One of the problems for the pupils has been that in such situations support teachers have often reverted to a model of teaching that they themselves experienced in school. Hence the phenomenon, observed by HMI (1989a), of support teachers engaging children in work that was conspicuously different from that of their peers and often unrelated to the main objectives that drove the class activities. Conflict can arise where efforts of the mathematics teacher, for example, to encourage thinking strategies, may be undermined by direct teaching based on personal experiences of the support teacher. Without joint planning and discussion, different objectives for teaching and different perceptions of the mathematics involved can generate confusion among the children and inhibit learning.

In terms of more generalization Stradling and Saunders (1993) concur with Dyson and Gains (1993) that there is a great need for SEN staff to take a much enhanced role in the whole-school management of effective learning provision. Involvement within departmental planning and co-ordination across departments would not only benefit the pupils involved but would raise the profile of special needs teachers as equal partners in the learning process. This could be effected in at least the two areas of organizational development and the management of change along with staff development and the management of personnel. These activities would allow the SEN teacher to be seen as someone concerned with raising the attainment of all pupils and not solely concerned with managing the 'problem' of Special Educational Need.

BIASED EXPECTATIONS AND DISCRIMINATION

Many of the processes of bias in the criteria of competence which may be seen to be applied in the case of learning difficulty are also gendered processes. The Assessment of Performance Unit Surveys conducted in the early 1980s revealed gender differences in achievement and attitudes: girls appeared to achieve less and have more negative attitudes to secondary school mathematics than boys. Spender (1981) showed that mathematics teachers may respond to boys and girls differently and ask them qualitatively different questions. Walden and Walkerdine (1982) showed girls superior performance in mathematics in the early years of schooling is attributed to rule following and rote learning by teachers. They extended this work in Walden and Walkerdine (1985) to show how boys were frequently entered for high-status public examinations despite poorer performance than girls who were excluded. Walkerdine (1988) argues that the gendered patterns of signification in secondary school mathematics classrooms privilege certain aspects of male behaviour. Male rule breaking for example may be read as evidence of the understanding and conceptual grasp not revealed in neat and careful work by girls which is read by teachers as being of lesser worth. Dweck *et al.* (1978) studied the ways in which teachers made gendered responses to children's work. They provide evidence of very different mathematical worlds for boys and girls which in themselves are suggestive of the findings of Walden and Walkerdine. Boys appeared to receive more frequent criticism than girls. However this criticism was more often referenced to their lack of effort or attentiveness rather than their mathematical ability. Reference was more likely to be to intellectual ability when boys did receive positive feedback. Girls were not seen to receive as much criticism as boys but when they did it carried with it messages of lack of ability rather than effort or attentiveness. The underlying message for boys is that if they work hard they will achieve whereas for girls it is that their performance in mathematics reveals their ability rather than the amount of effort they put into their work.

Classrooms such as those studied by Dweck *et al.* are those in which girls would become concerned to avoid the damaging effects of criticism of their ability and boys are provided with frequent prompts to try harder. Thus girls would tend to be careful to avoid breaking the rules for fear of the consequences. For boys making a mistake carries much less painful consequences. They are much more likely to take the risks that are identified by Walden and Walkerdine as the signifiers of 'real understanding' in secondary school mathematics classrooms. Here then is the suggestion of a cycle of teacher and learner behaviour which disadvantages girls. The Assessment of Performance Unit Surveys may, from this perspective, be taken as evidence of a cycle of social constructivism in mathematics.

Girls Into Maths Can Go (Burton, 1986) is a collection of perspectives on girls learning mathematics and attempts to propose strategies by which disadvantages for girls may be overcome. As is the case in so many aspects of classroom and school life evidence is that disadvantaging factors are often studied in isolation. There have been very few empirical studies of the gender by SEN interaction (see Cooper, Upton and Smith (1991) for a recent exception). At present it is difficult to say what the gendered patterns of communication are with respect to secondary pupils with learning difficulties. Indeed there is very little understanding of the processes by which children obtain extra support in mainstream classes as a function of gender. A small scale pilot study (Daniels *et al.*, forthcoming) revealed the following findings:

- Significant gender differences exist in numbers of children receiving extra support irrespective of the identification procedure.
- The effective reasons for referral reveal gender differences. These reasons are rarely made explicit if referral is made to agencies outside the school and in some cases, the classroom.
- Boys are often given forms of support which are not designed to meet the needs identified.

Thus it would seem that there are very good grounds for suspecting that the gender by SEN interaction in mathematics is one which deserves a good deal of attention. In policy terms a first response could be that of gender monitoring support practices. At a time when the level of available support is dwindling it is vital that whatever resources are at hand are used to maximum benefit. An examination of support practices from the perspective of gender raises the fundamental issue of the relationship between needs and provision. Special needs practices can easily become those in which real needs are 'reformulated' in terms of provision that is known to be available. For example aggressive behaviour on the part of boys may cause real concern to a classroom teacher. The only provision that is available may be for support for difficulty in reading. Whilst the boys may well experience difficulty with reading, the major classroom concern is with behaviour. Many such boys are placed in special provision that is not designed to meet their needs. It may meet the teacher's needs in that they may be withdrawn from the classroom. It may meet the school's needs in that it is seen to be making some response. There will be instances when their new-found skills help these boys to maintain a less 'prominent' position in the classroom. However, the practice of offering support with reading as a means of easing classroom behaviour difficulty is unlikely to be educationally or economically efficient. There is also the often ignored point that the practice of placing so many boys in reading support may be discriminating against girls who have needs that would benefit from such provision. The processes of gender differentiation would seem to operate at many levels within schools. They seek to discriminate against girls in the effective criteria of competence held by teachers and developed by pupils as a function of teacher attributions. They also seek to discriminate in SEN practices. Whilst these issues are not yet fully understood they would appear to be powerful and pervasive. It is ironic that whilst on the one hand 'mainstream' practices in mathematics are biased against girls, on the other hand SEN support practices also appear to be biased against girls. SEN support tends to concentrate on reading to the detriment of mathematics and thus the lot of the girl who is seen to be struggling in mathematics is not a happy one. There are no easy solutions to this complex set of problems.

At least one of the whole-school policy issues is clear. Following the Code of Practice requirement that a school's SEN policy should include 'criteria for monitoring the success of the school's policy' it would seem vital that the relationship between pupil need and provision offered is open to scrutiny.

These matters may then receive attention in the policy development *process* in the school. Schools need to know what is going on and then be able to introduce procedures that are designed to bring about improvements that are themselves open to evaluation and subsequent modification. Hart (1992) outlines three main strands of staff response to an SEN integration programme in his school. These responses would seem to provide a useful summary of what can happen when a whole school develops a response to diversity:

1. There is a willingness among staff to adapt their teaching approaches and expectations. This has been accompanied by growing confidence that they can teach pupils with an increasing diversity of need.
2. A strong belief exists that difficulties can be overcome.
3. A realisation has developed that different quantities and types of support may be required to achieve targets. The aim is always to enable pupils to enter fully into the curriculum and to minimise their dependence on additional support. (p. 34)

Without the benefits of a clear policy framework and strong policy development process, the individual teacher in the classroom will find it much more difficult to make an adequate response to all pupils.

Epilogue

We write this epilogue in the midst of yet another flurry of DFE circulars and Commission reports. Following the recommendations of the Dearing Report (Dearing, 1994) it would seem likely that the use of a ten-level scale at Key Stage 4 will be abandoned and that new ways will be sought of accrediting the achievements of those who are low attainers in mathematics. At Key Stage 3 the range of attainment levels will be broadened to include levels 1 and 2 and differentiation within levels will be addressed. This may lead to a decrease in the number of pupils who need exempting from the National Curriculum through the use of statements within the Code of Practice. It may just be that the use of the statement producing accountability stages of the Code of Practice are generally reduced in comparison with current practice.

We welcome the de-coupling of levels of attainment from age within Key Stages, yet retain a certain caution as to how the same attainment level will be handled at six and sixteen. Similarly, we share a concern about the Pupil Referral Units and the function they will come to serve. Above all we hope that real progress will be made towards a genuine matching of educational provision and practice to meet instructional need rather than vice versa as has so often been the case in the past. We look forward to the active involvement of all pupils in the negotiation of appropriate learning environments and caution those who favour a 'back to basics' approach in mathematics with the following quote in mind:

> There is evidence that the public focusing of attention on standards in school which his occurred in recent years has created pressure in some quarters for a 'back to basics' movement. This has encouraged some primary teachers and some teachers of low attaining pupils in secondary school to restrict their teaching largely to the attainment of computational skills . . .
>
> *An excessive concentration on the purely mechanical skills of arithmetic for their own sake will not assist the development of understanding in . . . other areas. It follows that the results of a 'back to basics' approach (as we understand the words) are most unlikely to be those*

which its proponents wish to see, and we can in no way support or recommend an approach of this kind.

(Cockcroft Report, DES 1982, para. 278)

What difference will all the recent requirements and centrally-derived advice make to the pupils experience of mathematics in class-rooms? It is possible for schools to find ways of complying with demands without really addressing the need to change but, as we have argued in this book, in the better schools progress will be achieved through collaboration between mathematics and SEN staff supported by whole-school policies.

The issues which we have explored in this book have been issues in mathematics education for some considerable time. They have remained issues despite the efforts of governmental and non-governmental agencies to bring about change. OFSTED (1993b) remind us that low achievers are still seen to make disappointingly little progress throughout the eleven to sixteen age range. In many secondary schools the 'curriculum machine' appears still to rumble on oblivious to the response of pupils. 'About a tenth of the schools made good use of their records to plan for classes and individuals. However, in most of the schools there was some inflexible planning in that the work already planned would be done whatever the assessment evidence' (OFSTED, 1993b, p. 18). Time spent on number work in many schools is still excessive and ineffective in that there is little evidence of improvement. Many secondary school pupils still get bored by excessive practice. Their errors are still not analysed in terms of the implications for further teaching. In almost all the schools observed during 1992–3 some teaching of mathematics is carried out by teachers with no initial qualifications or relevant experience or recent in-service training (INSET) in mathematics. Some of these non-specialists are insecure in subject and National Curriculum knowledge. They still tend to teach low-ability groups.

These issues are not new. HMI in 1993 find no better quote than one they used fourteen years earlier in 1979:

In the *Secondary Survey* (1979), HMI wrote:
The concern teachers feel if their pupils achieve poorly in computational arithmetic is understandable; but if the cure involved no more than stepping up practice on a narrow range of written calculating procedures the numeracy problem would already have been solved. Practice needs to be carefully controlled, and supplemented by:

(i) *improved diagnosis of pupils' individual difficulties;*
(ii) *a better appreciation of the role of language and oral work;*
(iii) *more effective use of the applications of the ideas, both in the world around and in other subjects in the school.*

These comments are still relevant today for Attainment Targets 3 to 5 as well as AT2 and for pupils in all phases.

> *(Aspects of Secondary Education in England,* HMSO, 1979, quoted in OFSTED, 1993b)

We recognize that there are many benefits for all learners in the pedagogic developments that are required when pupils with SEN are included in mathematics in mainstream schools. Teaching that is responsive to learner needs; that builds on pupil understanding; that respects individual contributions as the basis for negotiation of mathematical understandings, lies at the heart of our model for the way forward. The constructivist paradigm in which we locate our own position celebrates active learners rather than passive pupils, constructors of knowledge rather than receivers and above all individuals who have confidence to *use their own* mathematics. The control over these developments still remains, to a great extent, in the hands of teachers and schools.

References and suggested further reading

Ackerman, P.T., Anhalt, J.M. and Dykman, R.A. (1986) Arithmetic automization failure in children with attention and reading disorders: associations and sequels. *Journal of Learning Disabilities* 19(4), 222–32.

Ahmed, A. (1985) *Mathematics for Low Attainers: Some Classroom Activities and Approaches*. West Sussex Institute of Higher Education.

Ahmed, A. (1987) *Better Mathematics: A Curriculum Development Study*. London: HMSO.

Ahmed, A. (1989) 'Better expectations, better achievements'. In Widlake, P. (ed.) *Special Children Handbook: Meeting Special Needs Within the Mainstream School*. London: Hutchinson.

Ainley, J. (1988) 'Playing games and real mathematics'. In Pimm, D. (ed.) *Mathematics, Teachers and Children*. London: Hodder and Stoughton.

Ainscow, M. and Tweddle, D. (1979) *Preventing Classroom Failure*. London: Methuen.

Ainscow, M. and Tweddle, D. (1988) *Encouraging Classroom Success*. London: David Fulton.

Allardice, B. and Ginsburg, H.P. (1983) 'Children's psychological difficulties in mathematics'. In Ginsburg, H.P. (ed.) *The Development of Mathematical Thinking*. London: Academic Press.

Anghileri, J. (1985) Should we say 'times'? *Mathematics in School* 14(3), 24–6.

Anghileri, J. (1991) 'The language of multiplication and division'. In Durkin, K. and Shire, B. (eds) *Language in Mathematical Education*. Milton Keynes: Open University Press.

APU (1982) *Mathematical Development: Secondary Survey Reports Nos. 1–3*. London: HMSO.

APU (1989) *Communicating Mathematical Ideas: A Practical Interactive Approach At Ages 11 and 15*. London: HMSO.

Arnold, M. (1910) *Reports On Elementary Schools: 1852–82*. London: HMSO.

Ashman, A.F. and Elkins, J. (1990) 'Cooperative learning among special students. In Foot, H.C., Morgan, M.J. and Shute, R.H. (eds) *Children Helping Children*. London: Wiley.

Association of Metropolitan Authorities (1993) *Education Act 1993: A Critical Guide*. London: Association of Metropolitan Authorities.

Austin, J.D. (1982) Children with a learning disabilty and mathematics. *School Science and Mathematics* (March), 201–8.

Ausubel, D. (1968) *Educational Psychology: A Cognitive View*. New York: Holt, Rinehart and Winston.

Bangs, J. (1993) Support services – stability or erosion. *British Journal of Special Education* **20**(3), 105–8.

Barham, J. (1988) *Teaching Mathematics To Deaf Children*. Unpublished Ph.D. University of Cambridge.

Barham, J. and Bishop, A. (1991) 'Mathematics and the deaf child'. In Durkin, K. and Shire, B.(eds) *Language in Mathematical Education*. Milton Keynes: Open University Press.

Baroody, A.J. (1984) Children's difficulties in subtraction. Some causes and questions. *Journal for Research in Mathematics Education* **15**, 203–13.

Baroody, A.J. (1986) Counting ability of moderately handicapped children. *Education and Training of the Mentally Retarded* **21**, 298–300.

Baroody, A.J. and Hume, J. (1991) Meaningful mathematics instruction: the case of fractions. *Remedial and Special Education* **12**(3), 54–68.

Bartlett, D. and Peacey, N. (1992) Assessments and Issues for 1992. *British Journal of Special Education* **19**(3), 94–7.

Beilin, H. (1975) *Studies in the Cognitive Basis of Language Development*. New York: Academic Press.

Bennett, N. (1987) Changing perspectives on teaching and learning processes. *Oxford Review of Education* **13**(1).

Bennett, N., Desforges, C., Cockburn, A. and Wilkinson, B. (1984) *The Quality of Pupil Learning Experiences*. London: Lawrence Erlbaum.

Bidell, T.R. (1992) Beyond interactionism in contextualist models of development. *Human Development* **35**, 306–15.

Booth, L. (1984) *Algebra: Children's Strategies and Errors*. Windsor: NFER-Nelson.

Brennan, W. (1974) *Shaping the Education of Slow Learners*. London: Routledge and Kegan Paul.

Brennan, W. (1979) *Curricular Needs of Slow Learners. Schools Council Working Paper 63*. London : Evans/Methuen Educational.

Brennan, W. (1985) *Curriculum for Special Needs*. Milton Keynes: Open University Press.

Brownell, W.A. (1928) *The Development of Children's Number Ideas in the Grades*. Supplementary Educational Monograph No 35. Chicago: Chicago University Press.

Brownell, W.A. (1935) Psychological considerations in the teaching and learning of arithmetic. *The Teaching of arithmetic, The Tenth Yearbook of the National Council for Teachers of Mathematics*. New York: Teachers College, Columbia University.

Bruner, J.S. (1960) *The Process of Education*. Harvard: Harvard University Press.

Bruner, J.S. (1966) *Studies in Cognitive Growth*. New York: Wiley.

Bruner, J.S. (1967) *Towards a Theory of Instruction*. Cambridge, Mass: Belkuap Press.

Bruner, J.S. (1987) 'Prologue to English edition'. In Rieber, R.W. and Carton, A.S. (eds) *The Collected Works of L.S. Vygotsky: Problems of General Psychology*. London: Plenum Press.

Burton, L. (1984) *Thinking Things Through: Problem Solving in Mathematics*. Oxford: Basil Blackwell.

Burton, L. (ed.) (1986) *Girls Into Maths Can Go*. London: Cassell.

Buxton, L. (1981) *Do You Panic About Mathematics?* London: Heinemann.

Carraher, T.N., Carraher, D.W. and Schliemann, A.D. (1985) Mathematics in the streets and in schools. *British Journal of Developmental Psychology* **3**, 21–9.

Case, R. and Bereiter, P. (1984) From behaviourism to cognitive behaviourism to cognitive development: steps in the evolution of instructional design. *Instructional Science* **13**(2), 141–58.

Clarkson, J. and Galbraith, G. (1992) Bilingualism and mathematics learning: another perspective. *Journal for Research in Mathematics Education* **23**(1), 34–44.

Clements, M. (1980) Analyzing children's errors in written mathematical tasks. *Educational Studies in Mathematics* **11**(1), 1–21.

Cobb, P., Yackel, E. and Wood, T. (1992) A constructivist alternative to the representational view of mind in mathematics education. *Journal for Research in Mathematics Education* **23**(1), 2–33.

Cooper, B. (1985) *Renegotiating Secondary School Mathematics: A Study of Change and Stability*. London: Falmer Press.

Cooper, P., Upton, G. and Smith, C. (1991) Ethnic minority and gender distribution among staff and pupils in facilities for pupils with emotional and behavioural difficulties in England and Wales. *British Journal of Sociology of Education* **12**(1), 77–94.

Costello, J. (1991) *Teaching and Learning Mathematics 11–16*. London: Routledge.

Cummins, J. (1979) Linguistic interdependence and the educational development of bilingual children. *Review of Educational Research* **49**(2), 222–51.

Cummins, J. (1984) *Bilingualism and Special Education*. Clevedon: Multilingual Matters.

Daniels, H. (1988) Misunderstandings, miscues and mathematics. *British Journal of Special Education* **15**(1), 11–13.

Daniels, H. (1990) Number competence and communication difficulty: a Vygotskian analysis. *Educational Studies* **16**(1), 49–59.

Daniels, H. (ed.) (1993a) *Charting the Agenda: Educational Activity After Vygotsky*. London: Routledge.

Daniels, H. (1993b) Coping with mathematics in the National Curriculum: pupil strategies and teacher responses. *Support for Learning* **8**(2), 65–70.

Daniels, H. and Norwich, B. (1993) *Teacher Support Teams in Three Enfield Primary Schools: An Evaluation Report*. London: University of London, Institute of Education.

Daniels, H. and Ware, J. (eds) (1990) *Special Educational Needs and the National Curriculum, the Impact of the Education Reform Act*. Bedford Way series. London: University of London, Institute of Education.

Daniels, H., Norwich, B. and Anghileri, J. (1993) Teacher support teams: an evaluation of a school based approach to meeting special educational needs. *Support for Learning* **8**(4), 169–73.

Daniels, H., Hey, V., Leonard, D. and Smith, M. (forthcoming) Gender processes in special needs in mainstream schools. In Holland, J. (ed.) *Equality and Diversity*. Milton Keynes: Open University Press.

Dearing, R. (1993) *The National Curriculum and Its Assessment: Final Report*. London: SCAA.

Denvir, B. (1986) Understanding of number concepts in low attaining 7–9 year olds. *Educational Studies in Mathematics* **17**, 143–64.

Denvir, B. (1988) 'What are we assessing in mathematics and what are we assessing for?' in Pimm, D. (ed.) *Mathematics, Teachers and Children*. London: Hodder and Stoughton.

Denvir, B., Stolz, C. and Brown, M. (1982) *Low Attainers in Mathematics 5–16: Policies and Practices in Schools*. Schools Council Working Paper 72. London: Methuen.

Department for Education (1992) *Exclusions A Discussion Paper*. London: HMSO.

Department for Education (1994) *The Code of Practice*. London: HMSO.

Department of Education and Science (1970) *Education (Handicapped Children) Act 1970*. London: HMSO.

Department of Education and Science (1978) *Special Educational Needs (The Warnock Report)*, London: HMSO.

Department of Education and Science (1981) *The Education Act 1981*. London: HMSO.

Department of Education and Science (1982) *Mathematics Counts: Report of the Committee of Inquiry Into the Teaching of Mathematics in Schools (The Cockcroft Report)*. London: HMSO.

Department of Education and Science (1983) *Blueprint for Numeracy: An Employers Guide To the Cockcroft Report*. London: HMSO.

Department of Education and Science (1985) *General Certificate of Education: The National Criteria – Mathematics*. London: HMSO.

Department of Education and Science (1988) *National Curriculum Task Group On Assessment and Testing: A Report*. London: HMSO.

Department of Education and Science (1989a) *Discipline in Schools (The Elton Report)*. London: HMSO.

Department of Education and Science (1989b) *Non-Statutory Guidance To the National Curriculum in Mathematics*. London: HMSO.

DeStefano, J.S. (1984) 'Learning To Communicate in the Classroom'. In Pellegrini, A.D. and Yawbey, T.D. *The Development of Oral and Written Language in Social Contexts*. Norwood, N.J.: Ablex.

Dickson, L., Brown, M. and Gibson, O. (1984) *Children Learning Mathematics: A Teacher's Guide to Recent Research*. London: Cassell.

Dienes, Z. (1960) *Building Up Mathematics*. London: Hutchinson.

Dockrell, J. and McShane, J. (1993) *Children's Learning Difficulties: A Cognitive Approach*. Oxford: Blackwell.

Donlan, C. and Hutt, E. (1991) 'Teaching mathematics to young children with language disorders'. In Durkin, K. and Shire, B.(eds) *Language in Mathematical Education*. Milton Keynes: Open University Press.

Dowling, P. (1991) 'The contextualising of mathematics: towards a theoretical map'. In Harris, M. (ed.) *Schools, Mathematics and Work*. Brighton: Falmer Press.

Dowling, P. (1993) 'Theoretical totems: a sociological language for educational practice'. In Angelis, D. *et al.* (eds) *Political Dimensions in Mathematics Education: Curriculum Reconstruction for Society in Transition*. Cape Town: Cape Books.

Dweck, C.S., Davidson, W., Nelson, S. and Enna, B. (1978) 1: Sex differences in learned helplessness. 2: The contingencies of evaluative feedback in the classroom. 3: An experimental analysis. *Developmental Psychology* **14**, 268–76.

Dyson, A. and Gains, C. (1993) 'Special needs and effective learning: towards a collaborative model for the year 2000'. In Dyson, A. and Gains, C. (eds) *Special Needs in Mainstream Schools: Towards the Year 2000*. London: David Fulton.

Earp, W.N. and Tanner, F.W. (1980) Mathematics and language. *Arithmetic Teacher* 28(4), 32–4.

Edwards, A.D. and Westgate, D. (1987) *Investigating Classroom Talk*. London: Falmer Press.

Eisenhart, M., Borko, H., Underhill, R., Brown, C., Jones, D. and Agard, P. (1993) Conceptual knowledge falls through the cracks: complexities of learning to teach. *Mathematics for Understanding* 24(1), 8–40.

Ernest, P. (1986) Games. A rationale for their use in the teaching of mathematics in school. *Mathematics in School* 15(1).

Erting, C.J. (1985) Cultural conflict in a school for deaf children. *Anthropology and Education Quarterly*, 16, 225–43.

Evans, J. and Lunt, I. (1992) *Developments in Special Education Under LMS*. London: University of London, Institute of Education.

Fennema, E., Franke, M.L., Carpenter, T.P. and Carey, D.A. (1989) Using children's mathematical knowledge in instruction. *American Educational Research Journal* 30(3), 555–84.

Fleming, H., Dadswell, P. and Dodgson, H. (1990) Reflections on the integration of children with learning difficulties into secondary mathematics classes. *Support for Learning* 5(4).

Fletcher Campbell, F. with Hall, C. (1993) *LEA Support for Special Needs*. Slough: Nfer-Nelson.

Fuson, K.C. (1988) *Children's Counting and Concepts of Number*. New York: Springer–Verlag.

Gagné, R.M. (1965) *The Conditions of Learning*. New York: Holt, Rinehart and Winston.

GAIM (1988) *Graded Assessment in Mathematics: Mathematics Development Pack*. London: Macmillan.

Galloway, D. (1985) *Schools, Pupils and Special Educational Needs*. London: Croom Helm.

Galloway, D. and Goodwin, C. (1987) *The Education of Disturbing Children: Pupils with Learning and Adjustment Difficulties*. London: Longman.

Gilroy, A. and Moore, D.W. (1988) Reciprocal teaching of comprehension – fostering and comprehension – monitoring activities with ten primary school girls. *Educational Psychology* 8(1/2), 41–9.

Ginsburg, H.P. and Allardice, B.S. (1984) 'Children's difficulties with school mathematics.' In Rogoff, B. and Lave, J. (eds) *Everyday Cognition: Its Development in Social Context*. Cambridge, Mass: Harvard University Press.

Ginsburg, H.P. and Yamamoto, T. (1986) Understanding, motivation, and teaching: comment on Lamperts 'Knowing, doing and teaching mutiplication'. *Cognition and Instruction* 3(4), 357–70.

Goacher, B., Evans, J., Welton, J. and Wedell, K. (1988) *Policy and Provision for Special Educational Needs: Implementing the 1981 Act*. London: Cassell.

Good, T.L. and Brophy, J.E. (1984) *Looking in Classrooms*. 3rd Edition. New York: Harper and Row.

Greeno, J.G. (1986) Collaborative teaching and making sense of symbols: comment on Lamperts 'Knowing, doing and teaching multiplication',

Cognition and Instruction 3(4), 343–7.

Hansard Parliamentary Debates (1993) London: HMSO.

Harris, M. (ed.) (1991) *School, Mathematics and Work*. Brighton: Falmer Press.

Harris, M. and Evans, J. (1991) 'Mathematics and the work place'. In Harris, M. (ed.) *School, Mathematics and Work*. Brighton: Falmer Press.

Hart, K.M. (ed.) (1981) *Children's Understanding of Mathematics: 11–16*. London: John Murray.

Hart, K.M. (1992) Diversity at secondary level. *British Journal of Special Education* 19(1), 32–4.

Haylock, D. (1982) Understanding in mathematics: making connections. *Mathematics Teaching* No. 98.

Hembree, R. (1992) 'Research on calculators in mathematics education'. In Fey, J. and Hirsch, C. *Calculators in Mathematics Education*. Virginia: NCTM.

Hiebert, J. (1984) Children's mathematics learning: the struggle to link form and understanding. *Elementary School Journal* 84, 497–513.

HMI/Audit Commission (1992) *Getting in On the Act: Provision for Pupils with SEN: the National Picture*. London: HMSO.

HMI (1985) *Mathematics From 5 to 16*. London: HMSO.

HMI (1989a) *A Survey of Support Services for Special Educational Needs*. London: DES.

HMI (1989b) *A Survey of Pupils with Special Educational Needs in Ordinary Schools*. London: DES.

HMI (1989c) *Aspects of Primary Education: the Teaching and Learning of Mathematics*. London: DES.

HMI (1991) *The Implementation of the Curricular Requirements of the Education Reform Act: Mathematics: Key Stages 1 and 3; A Report By HM Inspectorate On the First Year, 1989–90*. London: HMSO.

HMI (1993) *The Integration of Pupils with Moderate Learning Difficulties Into Secondary Schools*. Ref 173/93/Ns. London: HMI/OFSTED.

Hofmeister, A.M. (1989) Teaching problem solving skills. *Educational Technology* 24(9), 26–9.

Holt, J. (1982) *How Children Fail*. 2nd Edition. London: Penguin.

Hughes, M. (1986) *Children and Number: Difficulties in Learning Mathematics*. Oxford: Basil Blackwell.

Hundeide, K. (1985) 'The tacit background of children's judgements'. In Wertsch, J.V. (ed.) *Culture, Communication and Cognition*. Cambridge: Cambridge University Press.

Hutchcroft, D.M.R. (1981) *Making Language Work*. London: Mcgraw-Hill.

Inner London Education Authority (1985) *Equal Opportunities for All? (The Fish Report)*. London: ILEA.

Isaacson, Z. (1987) *Teaching GCSE Mathematics*. London: Hodder and Stoughton.

Jaworski, B. (1988) 'Is' versus 'seeing as'. In Pimm, D. (ed.) *Mathematics, Teachers and Children*. London: Hodder and Stoughton.

Johnson, D.W. and Johnson, R.T. (1986) Mainstreaming and cooperative learning strategies. *Exceptional Children* 52(6) 553–61.

Jones, K. and Haylock, D.W. (1985) Developing children's understanding in mathematics. *Remedial Education*. 20(1), 30–4.

Kent Mathematics Project (KMP). London: Ward Lock Educational.

Kent, D. (1978) Some processes through mathematics is lost. *Educational Research* 21(1), 27-35.

Kibel, M. (1992) 'Linking language to action'. In Miles, T.R. and Miles, E. (eds) *Dyslexia and Mathematics*. London: Routledge.

Kilpatrick, J. (1987) 'What constructivism might be in education'. In Bergeron, J.C., Herscovicz, N. and Kieran, C. (eds) *Proceedings of the Eleventh Conference of the International Group for the Psychology of Mathematics Education*. Montreal: Université Montreal.

Kirkby D. (1992) *Games in the Teaching of Mathematics*. Cambridge: Cambridge University Press.

Klahr, D. and Wallace, J. (1973) The role of quantification operators in the development of conservation of quantity. *Cognitive Psychology* 4, 301-27.

Lampert, M. (1986) Knowing, doing and teaching multiplication. *Cognition and Instruction* 3(4), 305-42.

Larcombe, T. (1978) 'Mathematics 11-14'. In Hinson, M. (ed.) *Encouraging Results*. London: Macdonald Educational.

Larcombe, T. (1985) *Mathematical Learning Difficulties in the Secondary School: Pupil Needs and Teacher Roles*. Milton Keynes: Open University Press.

Lave, J. (1988) *Cognition in Practice: Mind Mathematics and Culture in Everyday Life*. Cambridge: Cambridge University Press.

Lemke, J. (1988) Genres, semantics and classroom education. *Linguistics and Education* 1, 81-99.

Leont'ev, A.N. (1981) *Problems of the Development of Mind*. Moscow: Progress Publishers.

Macnab, D.S. and Cummine, J.A. (1986) *Teaching Mathematics 11-16: A Difficulty Centred Approach*. Oxford: Basil Blackwell.

Mathematical Association (1968a) *Mathematics Projects in British Secondary Schools*. London: Bell.

Mathematical Association (1968b) *Mathematical Laboratories in Schools*. London: Bell.

Mathematical Association (1974) *Mathematics Eleven to Sixteen*. London: Bell.

Mathematical Association (1988) *Managing Mathematics: A Handbook for the Head of Department*. Cheltenham: The Mathematical Association and Stanley Thornes (Publishers) Ltd.

Mathematical Association (1992) *Computers in the Mathematics Curriculum*. Leicester: The Mathematical Association.

Mehan, H. (1978) 'Assessing children's language using abilities: methodological and cross-cultural implications'. In Armer, M. and Grimshaw, A.D. (eds) *Comparative Social Research: Methodological Problems and Strategies*. New York: Wiley.

Mehan, H. (1979) *Learning Lessons: Social Organisation in the Classroom*. Cambridge, Mass: Harvard University Press.

Mercer C. and Miller, S. (1992) Teaching students with learning problems in maths to acquire understanding and apply basic maths facts. *Remedial and Special Education* 13(3) (May/June).

Mevarech, Z.R. (1985) The effects of cooperative mastery learning strategies on mathematics achievement. *Journal of Educational Research* 78(6), 372-7.

Miles, T.R. (1983) *Dyslexia: The Pattern of Difficulties*. Oxford: Blackwell.

Miles, T.R. and Miles, E. (eds) (1992) *Dyslexia and Mathematics*. London: Routledge.

Mittler, P. (1992) Educational entitlement in the 90s. *Support for Learning* 7(4).

Moore, G. (1985) Calculators and remedial education in mathematics. *Remedial Education* 20(1).

National Curriculum Council (1989) *Implementing the National Curriculum– Participation By Pupils with Special Educational Needs*. (Circular No. 5). National Curriculum Council.

National Curriculum Council (INSET Resources) (1992) *Using and Applying Mathematics: Notes for Teachers at Key Stages 1–4*. National Curriculum Council.

National Curriculum Council (1993) *Special Needs and the National Curriculum: Opportunity and Challenge*. National Curriculum Council.

Newman, M. (1977) 'An analysis of sixth-grade pupils' errors in written mathematical tasks'. In Clements, S. and Foyster, M. *Research in Mathematics Education in Australia*.

Newman, D. Griffin, P. and Cole, M. (1989) *The Construction Zone: Working for Change in School*. Cambridge: Cambridge University Press.

Norwich, B. (1990a) 'Decision about special educational needs'. In Evans, P. and Varma, V. (eds) *Special Education: Past, Present and Future*. London: Falmer Press.

Norwich, B. (1990b) *Reappraising Special Needs Education*. London: Cassell.

Noss, R. (1991) 'The computer as cultural influence in mathematical learning'. In Harris M. (ed.) *Schools, Mathematics and Work*. Brighton: Falmer Press.

Nunes, T., Schliemann, A.D. and Carraher, D.W. (1993) *Street Mathematics and School Mathematics*. Cambridge: Cambridge University Press.

OFSTED (1993a) *Special Needs and the National Curriculum 1991–2: The Implementation of the Curricular Requirements of the Education Reform Act*. London: HMSO.

OFSTED (1993b) *Mathematics, Key Stages 1, 2, 3 and 4, Fourth Year 1992–3: The Implementation of the Curricular Requirements of the Education Reform Act – A Report From the Office of Her Majesties Chief Inspector of Schools*. London: HMSO.

OFSTED/Audit Commission (1992) *Getting in on the Act: Provision for Pupils with Special Educational Needs: The National Picture*. London: HMSO.

Palincsar, A.S. (1986) Metacognitive strategy instruction. *Exceptional Children* 53(2), 118–24.

Palincsar, A.S. and Brown, A.L. (1984) Reciprocal teaching of comprehension fostering and monitoring activities. *Cognition and Instruction* 1(2), 117–75.

Palincsar, A.S. and Brown, A.L. (1988) Teaching and practising thinking skills to promote comprehension in the context of group problem solving. *Remedial and Special Education* 9(1), 53–9.

Parmar, R.S. and Cawley, J.F. (1991) Challenging the routines and passivity that characterize arithmetic instruction for children with mild handicaps. *Remedial and Special Education* 12(5), 23–32.

Peter, M. (1993a) Editorial. *British Journal of Special Education* 20(2), 5.

Peter, M. (1993b) Address given at conference. *Special Educational Needs and the 1993 Act: The Impact of the Code of Practice*. 7 December 1993. London: University of London, Institute of Education.

Peterson, P.L , Fennema, E. and Carpenter, T. (1989) Using knowledge of how students think about mathematics. *Educational Leadership* (December 1988/January 1989), 42-6.

Piaget, J. (1952) *The Child's Conception of Number*. London: Routledge and Kegan Paul.

Piaget, J. (1953) How children form mathematical concepts. *Scientific American* (November).

Piaget, J. and Inhelder, B. (1958) *The Growth of Logical Thinking: From Childhood To Adolescence*. New York: Basic Books.

Pirie, S. and Kieren, T. (1992) Creating constructivist environments and constructing creative mathematics. *Educational Studies in Mathematics* 23, 505-28.

Pritchard, R.A., Miles, T.R., Chinn, S.J. and Taggart, A. T. (1989) Dyslexia and knowledge of number facts. *Links* 14(3), 17-20.

Randall, C. and Lester, F. (1982) *Teaching Problem Solving*. London: Edward Arnold.

Resnick, L.B. (1984) *Beyond Error Analysis: The Role of Understanding in Elementary School Arithmetic*. Pittsburgh: Pittsburgh University, Learning Research and Development Center.

Resnick, L.B. (1986) 'The development of mathematical intuition'. In Perlmutter M. (ed.) *Minnesota Symposium On Child Psychology* 19, Hillsdale, N.J.: Erlbaum.

Resnick, L.B. (1987) Learning in and out of school. *Educational Researcher* 16(9), 13-20.

Resnick, L.B. and Ford, W.W. (1981) *The Psychology of Mathematics for Instruction*. London: Lawrence Erlbaum.

Resnick, L.B., Nesher, P., Leonard, F., Magone, M., Omanson, S. and Peled, I. (1989) Conceptual bases of arithmetic errors: the case of decimal fractions. *Journal for Research in Mathematics Education* 20(1), 8-27.

Rieber, R.W. and Carton, A.S. (eds) (1987) *The Collected Works of L.S. Vygotsky: Problems of General Psychology*. London: Plenum Press.

Riley, M., Greeno, J. and Heller, J. (1983) 'Development of children's problem-solving ability in arithmetic'. In Ginsburg, H. (ed.) *The Development of Mathematical Thinking*. London: Academic Press.

Russell, R. and Ginsburg, H.P. (1984) Cognitive analysis of children's difficulties. *Cognition and Instruction* 1, 217-44.

Saxe, G.B. (1989) Transfer of learning across cultural practice. *Cognition and Instruction* 6(4) 331-66.

Saxe, G.B. (1991) *Culture and Cognitive Development: Studies in Mathematical Thinking*. New York: Erlbaum.

Saxe, G.B., Gearhart, M. and Guberman, S.R. (1984) 'The social organization of early number development'. In Rogoff, B. and Wertsch, J.V. (eds) *Childrens Learning in the Zone of Proximal Development*. San Francisco: Jossey-Bass.

Saxe, G.B., Gearhart, M., Note, M. and Paduano, P. (1993) 'Peer interaction and the development of mathematical understandings: a new framework for research and educational practice'. In Daniels, H. (ed.) *Charting the Agenda: Educational Activity After Vygotsky*. London: Routledge.

Saxe, G.B., Guberman, S.R. and Gearhart, M. (1988) Social processes in early number development. *Monographs of the Society for Research in Child Development* **52**(2).

SCAA (1994) *Mathematics in the National Curriculum Draft Proposals.* London: SCAA.

Schaeffer, B., Eggleston, V. and Scott, J. (1974) Number development in young children. *Cognitive Psychology* **6**, 357–79.

Schoenfeld, A.H. (1985) *Mathematical Problem Solving.* London: Academic Press.

Schoenfeld, A.H. (1988) When good teaching leads to bad results: the disasters of well taught mathematics courses. *Educational Psychologist* **23**, 145–66.

Schon, D. (1987) *Educating the Reflective Practitioner.* San Francisco: Jossey-Bass.

Shan, S.J. and Bailey, P. (1991) *Multiple Factors: Classroom Mathematics for Equality and Justice.* Stoke On Trent: Trentham Books.

Shuard, H. (1991) Mathematics and Pupils with Special Needs. Mimeo.

Shuard, H. and Rothery, A. (eds) (1984) *Children Reading Mathematics.* London: John Murray.

Simon, B. (1981) 'Why no pedagogy in England?' In Simon, B. and Tayor, W. (eds) *Education in the Eighties.* Andover: Batsford.

Skemp, R. (1971) *The Psychology of Learning Mathematics.* Harmondsworth: Penguin.

Skemp, R. (1976) Relational understanding and instrumental understanding. *Mathematics Teaching* **77**, 20–6.

Smith, F. (1971) *Understanding Reading.* New York: Holt, Rinehart and Winston.

Snow, R.E. and Yallow, E. (1982) 'Education and intelligence'. In Sternberg, R.J. (ed.) *Handbook of Human Intelligence.* Cambridge: Cambridge University Press.

Spender, D. (1981) *Invisible Women.* London: Writers and Readers Publishing Co-Operative.

Stigler, J.W. and Perry, M. (1990) 'Mathematics learning in Chinese, Japanese and American classrooms'. In Stigler J. W. *et al.* (eds) *Cultural Psychology: Essays on Comparative Human Development.* Cambridge: Cambridge University Press.

Stradling, R. and Saunders, L. (1993) Differentiation in practice: responding to the needs of all pupils. *Educational Research* **35**(2), 127–37.

Stradling, R. and Saunders, L. with Weston, P. (1991) *Differentiation in Action: A Whole School Approach for Raising Attainment.* London: HMSO.

Swann, W. (1985) Is the integration of children with special needs happening? An analysis of recent statistics of pupils in special schools. *Oxford Review of Education* **11**(1), 3–18.

Swann, W. (1988) 'Learning difficulties and curriculum reform: integration or differentiation? In *Planning for Special Needs: A Whole School Approach.* Thomas, G. and Feiler, A. (eds) Oxford: Blackwell.

Tateyama-Sniezek, K.M. (1990) Cooperative learning: does it improve the academic achievement of students with handicaps? *Exceptional Children* **56**(5), 426–37.

Thomas, G. (1993) 'Good behaviour. A review'. In *Times Educational Supplement* 11 June 1993, 14.

Thompson, D. and Barton, L. (1992) The wider context: a free market. *British Journal of Special Education* 19(1), 13–15.

Thomson, M. (1991) 'Mathematics and Dyslexia'. In Durkin, K, and Shire, B. (eds) *Language in Mathematical Education*. Milton Keynes: Open University Press.

Thorndike, E.L. (1913) *The Psychology of Arithmetic*. New York Teachers College.

Tomlinson, S. (1981) *Educational Subnormality: A Study in Decision-Making*. London: Routledge and Kegan Paul.

Tomlinson, S. (1985) The expansion of special education. *Oxford Review of Education* 12, 157–65.

Trickett, L. and Sulke, F. (1988) 'Low attainers *can* do mathematics'. In Pimm, D. (ed.) *Mathematics, Teachers and Children*. London: Hodder and Stoughton.

Vevers, P. (1992) Getting in on the act. *British Journal of Special Education* 19(2).

Vygotsky, L.S. (1978) *Mind in Society. The Development of Higher Psychological Processes*. Cambridge, Mass: Harvard University Press.

Walden, R. and Walkerdine, V. (1982) *Girls and Mathematics: The Early Years Bedford Way Papers No. 8*. London: University of London, Institute of Education.

Walden, R. and Walkerdine, V. (1985) *Girls and Mathematics: From Primary To Secondary Schooling Bedford Way Papers No. 24*. London: University of London, Institute of Education.

Walkerdine, V. (1988) *The Mastery of Reason: Cognitive Development and the Production of Rationality*. London: Routledge.

Webster, R.E. (1979) Visual and aural short-term memory capacity deficits in mathematics students. *Journal of Educational Research* 72(5), 277–83.

Wedell, K. (1990) 'The 1988 Act and current principles of special needs education: an overview'. In Daniels, H. and Ware, J. (eds) *The Implications of the National Curriculum for Children with Special Educational Needs*. London: Kogan Page.

Wedell, K. (1993a) Special needs education: the next 25 years. *National Commission On Education*. Briefing No. 14.

Wedell, K. (1993b) Address given at *Special Educational Needs and the 1993 Act: The Impact of the Code of Practice*. 7 December 1993. London: University of London, Institute of Education.

Weston, P., Barrett, E. and Jamison, J. (1992) *The Quest for Coherence: Managing the Whole Curriculum 5–16*. Slough: Nfer.

Williams, A. (1985) Towards numeracy. *Remedial Education* 20(1), 6–11.

Williams, A. (1990) Mathematics in transition. *British Journal of Special Education* 17(2), 57–60.

Wittrock, M. (1974) A generative model of mathematics learning. *Journal for Research in Mathematics Education* 5, 181–96.

Wood, D. (1988) *How Children Think and Learn*. Oxford: Basil Blackwell.

Wood, H.A., Wood, D.J., Kingsmill, M.C., French, J.R.W. and Howarth, S.P. (1984) The mathematical achievements of deaf children from different educational environments. *British Journal of Educational Psychology* 54, 254–64.

Name Index

Subject Index